CASE STUDIES IN
CULTURAL ANTHROPOLOGY

GENERAL EDITORS
George and Louise Spindler
STANFORD UNIVERSITY

¡QUÉ GITANO!

Gypsies of Southern Spain

IBERIAN PENINSULA

FRANCIA

OCEANO ATLANTICO

PYRENEES

ESPAÑA

CATALUÑA

Barcelona

PORTUGAL

Madrid

Córdoba

Sevilla

ANDALUCIA

Granada

Jerez

Málaga

Gibraltar

MAR MEDITERRANEO

Morocco

Gitanerías

Early Gypsy Migration Routes

¡QUÉ GITANO!

Gypsies of Southern Spain

By

BERTHA B. QUINTANA
Montclair State College

and

LOIS GRAY FLOYD
Montclair State College

CASE STUDIES IN CULTURAL ANTHROPOLOGY

HOLT, RINEHART AND WINSTON, INC.

NEW YORK   CHICAGO   SAN FRANCISCO   ATLANTA
DALLAS   MONTREAL   TORONTO   LONDON   SYDNEY

Cover: *Isabel*

DX
251
.Q55
PNP / X

With affectionate gratitude

to

AUGUSTA and WALTER STARKIE

who have generously shared
their fifty years of marriage
with the students, scholars,
and Gypsies of the world.

Foreword

About the Series

These case studies in cultural anthropology are designed to bring to students, in beginning and intermediate courses in the social sciences, insights into the richness and complexity of human life as it is lived in different ways and in different places. They are written by men and women who have lived in the societies they write about, and who are professionally trained as observers and interpreters of human behavior. The authors are also teachers, and in writing their books they have kept the students who will read them foremost in their minds. It is our belief that when an understanding of ways of life very different from one's own is gained, abstractions and generalizations about social structure, cultural values, subsistence techniques, and the other universal categories of human social behavior become meaningful.

About the Authors

Bertha B. Quintana was born in New York City and received her training in cultural anthropology at New York University. She has taught at New York University and Upsala College, and is presently Professor of Anthropology and Chairman of the Department of Anthropology at Montclair State College. Prior to the completion of her graduate studies, she was on the administrative staff of Vassar College. A specialist in the culture of the Gypsies of southern Spain, Dr. Quintana has conducted extensive fieldwork among the Gypsies of Granada. In 1959 she completed a study of the traditional themes and Deep Song of the Andalusian Gypsies (the subject of her doctoral dissertation), and in 1961, 1963, 1965, 1966, 1968, 1969, and 1970 she returned to Granada to study Gypsy enculturative/acculturative adaptations in the context of cultural change. In addition to her work in Spain, Dr. Quintana has spent time in West Africa where, on professional assignment for New York University in 1960, she studied Ghanaian educational problems. Since 1966 Dr. Quintana's fieldwork has been conducted in collaboration with her colleague Lois Gray Floyd, a psychologist. Their interdisciplinary focus has been on individuation and stress in contemporary Andalusian Gypsy culture, changing aspirations, and minority/majority accommodation patterns. Dr. Quintana is a Fellow of the American Anthropological Association, the Society for Applied Anthropology, the American Sociological Society, and the Gypsy Lore Society.

Lois Gray Floyd (Mrs. William Floyd, 2nd) was born in Iowa and received her graduate training in psychology at the University of Texas and New York University. She has taught at the University of Texas, New York University, and Long Island University. Dr. Floyd is a specialist in ethnopsychology and social psychology. Her focus on transcultural research has taken her to Karachi, Pakistan

(1957), Saigon, Vietnam (1959), and Tokyo, Japan (1964). In 1966, 1968, and 1970 she completed a study among Granada's Sacro Monte Gypsies of perception and the achievement need, and she has been engaged since that time in related interdisciplinary research. Dr. Floyd is a member of the American Psychological Association and the American Anthropological Association. Together, Drs. Floyd and Quintana teach interdisciplinary courses in psychological anthropology at Montclair State College. They made a return trip to Granada in the summer of 1971.

About the Book

To anyone who has traveled in Spain and seen the Gypsies of Andalusia in their Sacro Monte caves, or engaged in flamenco dancing and singing in hotels and nightclubs, or encountered small nomadic caravans along the road, this study rings true. Gypsy culture has been a subject of great interest in the Western world for centuries. Gypsies and Gypsy ways have been written about, praised, disparaged, legislated against, and supported by patrons, but social scientists have made few serious studies of them and their way of life. The authors of this case study, an anthropologist and a psychologist, are to be praised both for their attention to the historical dimension of Gypsy culture and for their ability to observe directly and interview relevantly.

This case study moves from the general to the particular and back to the general. It is about Gypsy culture in the more abstract sense of cultural themes and history as well as about individual Gypsies and their responses in particular situations. It deals with the romantic and creative aspects of Gypsy culture, but it also provides insight into the immediate problems of existence faced by a people who have lived by their wits and by their art in a frequently very hostile environment. It is unique not only because anthropological and psychological methods and interpretations are combined and because history, cultural themes, and Gypsies as living people are dealt with, but also because we are treated to that rare event in ethnography—when the people studied state their views of the culture of the ethnographer. That the views are not entirely flattering gives the reader a better understanding of both Andalusian Gypsies and American culture.

Though the authors are clearly deeply impressed by the quality and vitality of traditional Gypsy culture, they are also concerned with the ways in which it is changing and adapting in response to contemporary pressures. But in their change, still, Gypsies do not become uniform or ordinary. They continue to view themselves as separate from others. This sense of separateness is something important for all of us to understand since it is in this sense that human beings have always found their pasts and their futures.

GEORGE AND LOUISE SPINDLER
General Editors

Introduction
by Walter F. Starkie

Ramón Perez de Ayala, one of the most distinguished novelists of the modern Spanish literary Renaissance, once said that Spain is the only country whose inhabitants have merged so harmoniously with the Romany race that Gypsy and Spanish tradition coincide with one another. Imagine Granada without its legendary "Kings of the Mountain," as the Gypsies of the Sacro Monte are known. For centuries Romanies were persecuted all over Europe: They were accused of cannibalism; they were treated as slaves and chained up like dogs. But here in Granada their mountain of caves became a national monument—a pendant, as it were, to the Alhambra. Ever since, they have been paid to cast their glamor upon moneyed tourists and to perpetuate the romantic Spain which was consecrated by the picturesque writing of Washington Irving, De Amicis, and Gautier.

This monograph, based upon research done in Andalusia with special reference to Granada and the Sacro Monte during the years 1959–1970, is a scholarly contribution to anthropological studies. It is all the more valuable because it analyzes the life of the sedentary Gypsies of the Sacro Monte at the crucial moment of transition between pre–Civil War Granada and the Granada of recent years. During the earlier period Granada was dominated by the composer Manuel de Falla and his disciple, the poet Federico García Lorca, who, as a result of the Festival of Deep Song (*Cante Jondo*, primitive Andalusian song) in 1922, made the Albaicín and the Sacro Monte the Mecca of writers, painters, and musicians.

My earliest memories go back fifty years to 1921, when my wife and I visited Granada on our honeymoon with an introduction to Falla from his friend Unamuno in Salamanca. Every evening during our stay in the city was spent with the composer and his sister in their *carmen* (villa) near the Alhambra. After playing for us his evocative *Noches en los Jardines de España*, he led us out into the moonlight along an avenue lined with cypress trees into the paradise of myrtle, boxwood, and laurel of the Generalife—"the palace of the Tone-Architect," as the Moors called it. Our senses were lulled by the murmuring cascades, while above our heads the nightingales were trilling and fluting in full-throated minstrelsy. Falla was then organizing with his friends, the painters Zuloaga and Rodriquez Acosta, the Festival of Deep Song, which was to take place the following year in the Plaza de los Aljibes on the Alhambra hill. It was at that festival I met for the first time the composer's young disciple, Federico García Lorca, who was to be a close friend of mine in the Residencia de Estudiantes in Madrid in the years 1924–1929 and later on in the years of the Republic, when his caravan theatre, La Barraca, with its strolling players, played in the pueblos of Spain. There is no doubt that the continued presence in Granada of the composer of *El Amor Brujo* and the author of *El Romancero Gitano* raised the prestige of the *gitanos* (Gypsies) of the Sacro Monte to its highest pitch, for poets, musicians, painters, and dancers from abroad flocked to the caves, attracted by exotic *zambras* (revelries) that seemed to bridge the centuries.

To the Romany historian the choice of Granada for the Festival of Deep Song was significant, for it was to Granada that the Gypsies, who belonged to the Original Band, eventually came in the fifteenth century; they established themselves beyond the Albaicín in the caves of the Sacro Monte, where they still dwell. And there is the ancient tradition that when Ferdinand and Isabel were besieging the Moors in the Alhambra fortress, the Gypsy smiths of the caves forged the projectiles that enabled the monarchs to capture the stronghold and the Kingdom of Granada in 1492. As a result of their good services they were given by the people of Granada, who had learned to respect their skills as metalworkers, the local privilege of being called "New Castilians" to differentiate them from their undisciplined nomadic brethren, who were called *gitanos bravíos* (wild Gypsies).

In *El Cante Jondo: Cante Primitivo Andaluz,* an important pamphlet which Falla wrote in Granada in 1922 to serve as an explanatory introduction to the Festival of 1922, he emphasized that the first Gypsy tribes which settled in Granada in the fifteenth century were those which introduced a new element into primitive Andalusian music (1950:121–147). Deep Song, he maintained, was a musical style growing out of an Andalusian foundation which fused with Byzantine liturgical, Arab, and Gypsy elements.

The question of *cante jondo*, however, is one that has always aroused controversy in Andalusia because of the rival schools of thought that exist among the aficionados or connoisseurs of flamenco. Sevilla too looks upon itself as the Mecca of *cante*, and with reason, for its Gypsy *zambras* in the district of Triana rivaled those of Córdoba, which still preserved the faint memory of the peerless Ziryab, "The Blackbird of Song." Ziryab, a favorite of the Caliph Hārūn Ar-Rashīd in Bagdad, migrated to Córdoba after the caliph's downfall and became even more famous at the court of the Emir Abdar-Rahmān II than he had been in the city of the Arabian Nights. Also in the triangular region of Andalusia, called in classical days the Elysian Field with its river Guadalete (or river of oblivion) stand the celebrated centers of *cante*—Cádiz, San Fernando, and Jerez de la Frontera, which were the haunts of many of the great singers of the past.

In the years 1933–1936, when I wandered all over Andalusia preparatory to the publication of *Don Gypsy* (1937), I spent even more time in the *cañada* [dell] *de los gitanos de Guadix* than I did in the Sacro Monte, for the Gypsies of Guadix were closer to the primeval Romanichals than their more sophisticated brethren of Granada. Whereas most of the latter were tainted with foreign notions imported from the tourist world of flamenco parody, the former were still unaffected by modern civilization. Their caves in the loam hills of Benalúa were haunts of Kobolds—a *Nibelheim* conjured up by the sun from the depths of the earth.

When I revisited the Sacro Monte in the years after the Civil War (1936–1939), I noticed a great change in the cave communities. Many of my old friends, such as Cabezuela and Cagachin, had passed on, and the world of flamenco parody had banished many of the ancient traditions of *cante jondo*. Some of the Gypsy cave dwellers had become capitalists, such as Lola Medina, the wealthy dancer and *capitana* who had enlisted the services of a well-known Madrid architect to fashion a sophisticated mansion out of her cave and to furnish it with illuminated alabaster baths and cocktail bars! Lola, a plain-looking girl whom I had seen dancing twelve years before in Cagachin's cave, was now a glamorous Gypsy "princess" wearing diamond rings and bracelets. She was a generous hostess to the invading foreign tourists, but I missed the *castizo* (noble, pure) spirit of the *zambras* of former days, when singers and dancers struggled with their *duende* (souls).

I recalled the vision of Carmen Amaya, the *gitana* of legend, with her wild mouth, flaring nostrils, coarse jet hair, and narrow glinting eyes that told the tale of centuries of fierce living that had characterized her race. She too was born in the caves, a flaming relic of the tribes whose *duende* was flitting away from Granada. In the dancing of Spanish Gypsies, such as the divine Pastora Imperio and Carmen Amaya, we noticed at times flashes of wildness and rebelliousness which recalled the *gitanos bravíos,* the outcasts against whom the Pragmatic Sanction of 1499 was directed. The dancing of the *cuadro flamenco* (team of flamenco performers) made us visualize the Spanish nomads still roaming today through the Sierra Morena and the Sierra Nevada, sleeping in the dried-up beds of rivers in the summer, or else camping in precarious caves which they burrow like rabbits in the loam hillsides.

As examples, let me describe two models of Gypsy personality which are most vividly impressed upon my mind: Pastora Imperio, the dancer, and Rafael el Gallo, the bullfighter. To describe the dancer I have only to quote the tribute Jacinto Benavente, Spain's greatest dramatist, once said about her artistry:

> Her flesh burns with the consuming heat of all eternity, but her body is like the very pillar of the sanctuary, palpitating as it is kindled in the glow of sacred fires. . . . When we watch Pastora Imperio life becomes more intense. The loves and hates of other worlds pass before our eyes and we feel ourselves heroes, bandits, hermits assailed by temptation, shameless bullies of the tavern—whatever is highest and lowest in one. . . . Finally, in a burst of exaltation we praise God, because we believe in God while we look at Pastora Imperio, just as we do when we read Shakespeare (Quoted in Starkie 1958:100).

As for Rafael el Gallo, I would refer to the tribute I paid him in a previous work (1953). In spite of the dazzling qualities of Joselito, admittedly the greatest *torero,* the true Gypsy *Faraón* was his elder brother Rafael, who even in his old age remained the most perfect example of the Gypsy aristocrat in the world. If I were asked to name one individual who personified Spanish Gypsy integrity, I would without a moment's hesitation choose Rafael el Gallo. He was good-hearted, affectionate, and generous to the extent that he became a Simple Simon at the mercy of every "sharper," in spite of his flamenco intelligence. Compassionate toward the misfortunes of others, he was nevertheless incapable of managing his own affairs, and it was only the ever-watchful kindness of friends like Belmonte that enabled him to weather his stormy career as bullfighter. For Rafael was the supreme example of the unstable, contradictory nature of the Gypsy. Nobody was more loudly acclaimed by the public and aficionados than that thoroughbred Gypsy who from childhood possessed intuitively the science and wisdom of the ancient art, and was unrivaled for his sudden flashes of genius, his brilliant improvisations. When writing of his great qualities, the priests of the Mithraistic caste described them lyrically, as they would the roulades and trills of a prima donna or the cantabile of a great violinist. But Gallo was a Gypsy and was never ashamed to admit that he was afraid; for fear (*jindama*), he would say, was due to evil spirits that cross the path of man, and therefore was not the result of any personal inferiority. Rafael el Gallo knew that these *malos mengues* might descend upon him at any moment, even in the open plaza before thousands of spectators, who had applauded him to frenzy the day before and given him two ears and the tail of the last bull he had killed. On one occasion in the bullring of Sevilla, after dedicating his second bull to the Capitán-General with as much regal dignity and composure as if he had been Duke of Little Egypt, he noticed a queer glint in the bull's eye and there and then refused to kill the animal. Neither the persuasiveness of his friends nor the threats of the Capitán-General were able to shake his resolve, so he was carried off by the police to jail.

I was particularly fascinated by the chapters describing our authors' field trips and interviews conducted in Granada and various Andalusian cities which are devoted to such themes as Gypsy freedom, loyalty, and fatalism. How poignant is the portrait of Isabel, celebrated as "La Golondrina," "the swallow," the eldest daughter of Joaquín, the head of the Fajardo-Maya tribe of Gypsies in the Sacro Monte. When asked if she became *la capitana* as her parents grew older, Isabel replied,

> No, but because I am the oldest. . . . My mother [the original Golondrina] had only two daughters. I, the oldest, have not only my art but also an ability to be with people. . . . So, as my mother grew older, she said, "Isabel, you put yourself at the center of the business," . . . and that is where I am—in the foreground . . . where I'll probably be until I die. . . . But I am *not* the captain. The captain is my father.

La Golondrina lives through these pages and fills with retrospective melancholy those of us who remember her dramatic dancing in the Duchess of Lécera's garden in the moonlight—a ghostly experience, for the ghost of Falla seemed to hover in the background. It was in that *carmen* that he spent his latter years before departing for South America. In that *carmen* I had visited him frequently in 1935 and heard him play parts of his last work, *La Atlántida*. La Golondrina (Isabel's mother) was the most attractive *capitana* I have ever known, and a pleasing contrast to the crafty La Coja, whose caves I had visited a decade before.

In 1963, when Bertha Quintana paid a return visit to the Fajardo-Maya Gypsies, she found the whole Sacro Monte in great trouble owing to the winter floods. She then became acquainted with Carolina, a fourteen-year-old *gitana* whose family had been drowned, and that friendship led her to investigate the celebrated schools founded by Padre Manjón in 1889. In the history of Spanish education no nobler pioneer can be found than that Apostle of the Gypsies, who was so devoted to the ragged children of the Albaicín and Sacro Monte that he founded a school for them in the caves. As the years went by, the school began to grow and grow until it evolved into the vast buildings of the Escuelas del Ave-María—a celebrated institution in Spain. Padre Manjón's name was already proverbial when I visited Granada in 1921. One image I have of the aged pastor remains engraved in my mind's eye. I came across him mounted on a white donkey as he ambled down the cactus-lined paths from the caves. I had met him originally through the British Vice-Consul of Granada, Victor Davenhill, an eccentric and a donkey lover like the padre, who used out-of-office hours to roam through the sierra on his dapple, consorting with the smugglers and Gypsies he chanced to meet. According to Davenhill, it was the saintly Father Manjón who prodded the Romanichals into activity with their beaten ironwork and copperwork, with the result that a prosperous industry soon developed in Granada.

It was the example set in the old days by such pastors as Padre Manjón that culminated in the pilgrimage of the Gypsies to Rome in September 1965 to ask the protection of the pope for their nomadic way of life. Once before, five-and-a-half centuries ago, in 1422, one of the Original Band which migrated into western Europe claimed to have reached Rome and received from the pontiff letters bidding the authorities in the countries through which the Gypsies wished to pass to treat with kindness and charity those nomads on their seven years of "penitential pilgrimage." Pope Paul VI, in his address of September 26, 1965, to 2000 Gypsies from southern, eastern, and western Europe, demonstrated to the world the respect which he felt Gypsies deserve. He addressed them as "dearest Nomads," telling them that they were perpetual pilgrims, "refugees always on the road." He referred to the terrible persecution the Gypsies had undergone and to the deliberate attempt to exterminate them under the Nazi regime. He assured them that a change had taken place in human society since the years when Gypsies had been made to suffer so cruelly. The Gypsies, in grateful tribute to the Holy Father, gave an impromptu *zambra* with violins, guitars, accordions, and gaily skirted dancing girls under Pope Paul's window in the Vatican.

As a result of the pope's sympathetic attitude, the status of Gypsies ameliorated in Italy, France, and Spain, and this has led to the creation of some new experimental schools in the West for Gypsies. Other churches followed the pope's example in Protestant countries, such as in Holland, under the auspices of the International Christian Movement. As our authors show, the humanization of the Catholic Church's attitude toward Granada's Gypsies has increased since the death of Padre Manjón. It has produced a gradual Gypsy response which has accelerated in recent years, owing to the help given to the poverty-stricken families driven from their caves by the floods of 1963. Younger and more progressive priests have brought assistance to the inhabitants of La Chana, the new *barrio*, and the attention of Spaniards has been focused on Gypsies by the founding of the Department of Social Service for Gypsies in Madrid. Nevertheless, our authors' interviews with La Chana's Gypsies do not substantiate the pope's optimism in 1965, certainly as far as Granada's *gitanos* are concerned. The older residents, our authors report, continue to look upon the caves of the Sacro Monte as their real home, and they bitterly resent that what they had thought to be a temporary move has become permanent. They blame corrupt officials for not repairing the damaged caves and the local residents of Granada for their selfish greed in using the Sacro Monte for touristic purpose alone. "Gypsy families . . . ," the authors state, "continue to suffer from hunger, and our small gifts of money to children more frequently than not were used for bread, rice, and milk for the family table rather than for the ice cream for which they were intended."

Several of the Gypsy informants with whom our authors worked in Andalusia —dancers, singers, guitarists—were brought to the 1964–1965 World's Fair in New York to give performances at the Spanish Pavilion. Thus, by a reversal of roles they became students of the American way of life for six months, and it is of interest to note how uncompromisingly critical they were of America during their stay, voicing comments such as: "All Americans do is make money. They know little about how to live." Americans "have many laws, but no law." It is characteristic of the cave-dwelling *gitanos* and *gitanas* not to allow themselves to be dazzled by the glamor of foreign life, which they regard as inferior to the enclosed life of their Gypsy community. They shrugged off the television sets and other modern conveniences as dispensable in comparison with the "real" things that matter in life, adding that Americans are too serious and forget the joy of life. A *gitana* in Granada said, "Gypsies don't always have enough food to eat . . . , but, even so, they never lack *alegría*. What is best about Gypsy life is its joy. This they will never lose."

Hearing the *gitanos* in New York expressing their nostalgia for their Sacro Monte caves, I was reminded of the reminiscences of La Chata, one of the dancers who electrified Paris at the Exhibition of 1889, and of whom the poet Catulle Mendès wrote:

> *Petites Gitanas farouches*
> *Dont l'oeil flambe ainsi qu'un couteau,*
> *Vous avez au flanc du coteau*
> *Pour palais des cavernes louches.*

He described the flight of these "bright-feathered birds" from their dark nests to "la Ville Lumière" and how the impresario who drew up the contract for them had immense trouble in persuading them to leave their beloved Granada. But La Chata and her comrades would not hear of the journey at all unless they were allowed to bring with them their fathers, mothers, brothers, sisters, and even their donkeys.

The character of the Gypsy dancers from the Sacro Monte has changed little, despite the Civil War, floods, and tourism; and Isabel, the heroine of our authors' monograph, possesses the same qualities of *chachipeñi romí* (genuine Gypsy woman) as La Chata, La Macarrona, and all those stars of the Gypsy dance of whom the celebrated German art critic Meier Graefe once wrote: "Among them the genius of the dance runs riot, not talent, but genius. One distinguishes them immediately . . . and recognizes a superior species in them."

WALTER F. STARKIE
President, The Gypsy Lore Society

Acknowledgments

Aside from those whose contributions will be more fully identified in the overview, our special gratitude is offered to Ethel J. Alpenfels, Peggy Anderson, Elisabeth S. Atkinson, Harriet Fitzgerald, William Floyd 2nd, Kathleen M. Lewis, and Ruth and Salvador Quintana. In various ways they endorsed our passports to the Gypsies of Spain over the years spanned by this work. To the Montclair State College Faculty Development Fund we are indebted for a grant which helped us to conduct our 1968 field study in Granada. We wish also to express our thanks to George and Louise Spindler for their helpful suggestions during the preparation of the manuscript. Their letters of encouragement were perfectly timed, one even reaching us in a Gypsy cave!

The generous and sensitive assistance of Manuela Escamilla, Francisco García Lorca, and Sofia Novoa is reflected in the Spanish side of our Gypsy mirror, as is that of the late Manuel Centeno and Doña Rosario, the Duchess of Lécera. To Fernán Casares and Rosa Duran, who have dedicated their lives to the preservation of Gypsy flamenco arts, we extend our appreciation for providing us with substance and inspiration. Both are evident in the photograph of Rosa Durán, *primera bailaora* of Madrid's *Zambra*, which we print (see page 54) with their gracious permission. The dedication of this book is an inadequate expression of gratitude to Augusta and Walter F. Starkie, while our thanks to the many *gitanos* who walked the Gypsy way with us can only be felt, not measured. We acknowledge our debt to them, and our inability to repay it.

BERTHA B. QUINTANA
LOIS GRAY FLOYD

Contents

Overview

THIS BOOK is about the Gypsies of Andalusia, a region in southern Spain. The choice of Andalusia was based on the fact that it has been regarded throughout the centuries as the dominant Gypsy "stronghold" in Spain. Accordingly, the culture of its Gypsy inhabitants may be considered to be representative of Spanish sedentary Gypsies in general, albeit increased tourism has operated greatly to accelerate the acculturative process in the decade spanned by the field studies reported in this work. Our focus is principally on the sedentary Gypsies of Granada, some of whom have continued to occupy the cave dwellings of Granada's Sacro Monte (Sacred Mountain) for more than five centuries. Descendants of the Gypsy tribes who settled in Andalusia, and who adapted themselves to Andalusian civilization, these Gypsies (*gitanos*)[1] are differentiated from other Gypsy inhabitants of southern Spain primarily in that they are not nomadic. In addition, many of our informants are Gypsies engaged in the performing flamenco arts, a fact which distinguishes them occupationally and economically from other sedentary Gypsies. Although the current popularity of flamenco music has drawn the best of the dancers, singers, and guitarists away from the Sacro Monte, those who remain continue, sometimes under extreme duress, to perpetuate their traditional ways of life.

Why Study Gypsies?

The question "Why study Gypsies?" is frequently asked by our students. It would be misleading to answer it in purely academic terms. Personal interest,

---

[1] See Glossary for definition of Spanish or Gypsy terms.

1

opportunities not necessarily of one's own making, and the interest evinced by colleagues and students in the topic throughout the years, all have played roles of varying importance in the selection process. *La dicha* (Gypsy luck)—for example, the chance encounter with Walter Starkie, president of the Gypsy Lore Society, at New York University in 1958—also helped to shape and direct what has since become both a professional and affectionate concern for a people whose cultural tenacity and integrity is too little known.

Each of the seven field trips out of which this book has evolved has had distinct purposes not the least of which was to create cultural awareness of a people whose culture is not only an ancient one but a living, changing one as well. Someone has said that to create cultural awareness is the rightful task of the anthropologist. Such an aim need not be immediately practical so long as it helps to achieve what Spindler refers to as "a more universalistic understanding of human life" (1955:6). But prolonged involvement in the life of a people gives rise to questions which transcend the purely descriptive reporting of that life style. How have Gypsies survived in the face of overwhelming historical "odds," inhuman persecution, laws aimed at their cultural extinction?—a question of significance for all minority peoples lacking both power and numbers in a world rapidly closing in on them. How do people withstand pressures aimed at their total assimilation, assuming that the desire for cultural preservation is at least as strong among them as the desire for change? And how can the demand for cultural uniqueness be harmoniously balanced against the uniformity of rising aspirations and wants? For no society puts all of its eggs on one side of the cultural scale, and no people in the contemporary world fail to share with other people a certain commonness of goals, needs, and wants. We do not answer all of these questions in this work. Indeed, many of the experiences it reports helped us to learn to ask them only. Yet, imperfect though our questions and tentative answers may be, work with Andalusian Gypsies has yielded data relative to the transmission and perpetuation of traditional culture themes, the process of enculturation, the function of oral tradition in a living culture, and, more recently, cultural change, individuation, and stress. It is to these areas of interest and concern that this book addresses itself.

How Do You Get In?

Because of the highly personalized nature of Gypsy relationships, relationships which almost entirely exclude the stranger, it was found that initial contact making was best facilitated through personal introductions effected through persons previously known and respected by the Gypsies. By way of example, in Granada, where we have subsequently enjoyed prolonged and intimate contact with the Fajardo-Maya Gypsies of the Sacro Monte, initial contact was made through the courtesy of the late Duchess of Lécera, their patroness and friend of long standing. While incipient Gypsy hospitality there was extended on the basis of the rather erroneous assumption that they shared the same "patroness" in common with an anthropologist, the deepening and continuation of this relationship was the outgrowth of prolonged, face-to-face (or knee-to-knee!) dialogues. The ethnologist was indeed more interviewed than interviewing.

Once in, Then What?

Utilizing the participant/observation techniques by which, to paraphrase Hoebel (1966:8), cultural anthropologists earn their ethnographic "spurs," the earliest materials collected in the study of Andalusian Gypsy culture consisted of field notes and photographs. In the beginning, the unstructured interview was found to yield the most satisfactory results. Data collected while simultaneously holding babies, sharing a meal, or witnessing a *zambra* (revelry) provided the necessary bases for the subsequent development of written interview guides. As rapport developed between ourselves and our informants, life history materials were tape-recorded and the introduction of standardized devices was facilitated. Indeed, as many of our informants were performing Gypsies engaged in various flamenco enterprises, the use of cameras and tape recorders was almost too readily accepted by them! Even after a decade of work among them, it is very doubtful that they care about the uses to which their accounts of themselves may be put, process rather than purpose being their primary concern.

Following the *Patrin*

Throughout the centuries, Gypsy use of secret signs, the *patrin*, has enabled them to effectively direct and guide the movements and actions of those who follow. For example, according to Clébert, a simple sign of the cross (†), perhaps scratched on a fence post, translates among them to warn "Here they give nothing"; a triangle with a horizontal line through it (△) communicates "The master just died"; and so on (1963:198–200). Just as the Gypsies have used this system of communication and "mutual aid" in the pursuit of their life purposes, so too have we followed the *patrins* of colleagues whose works suggested orientations and approaches to various aspects of this study. In advice and in published scholarship, we would symbolize them with the sign of a circle (O) to denote, as it does among Gypsies, "generous people."

The work of the late Robert Redfield, including his well-known folk society concept (1947) and his study of folk "moral order" as seen in technological perspective (1957), were found to be especially relevant to those areas of this book which address themselves to both traditionalism and innovation in Gypsy culture. Utilizing Morris Opler's concept of "themes in culture," we were able to identify important affirmations upon which Gypsy culture is based, and to study their modification over an eleven-year period. According to the Opler *patrin*, cultural themes are declared or implied postulates or positions, tacitly approved or openly promoted in a society, which find their expression in behavior, activities, and artifacts (1945:198–206). Cultural integration is achieved by the balancing of themes, some of which support and some of which limit other themes in the culture. The contrasting and mutual actions of themes one upon the other prevent, in most instances, the chance of any one theme "running away with the culture." In other words, there is a certain point–counterpoint quality about their operation. Like a multiple-armed seesaw, any one theme tends to balance the others out, to exert alternate pressures in providing a sense of order and rhythm to their combined operation. While weight distributions may vary, causing one to dip lower or higher than another, in the main, the overall interplay of cultural themes is complementary and supportive. Cultures differ, of course, in how much as well as in what kinds of order and rhythm operate. The thematic content of Gypsy culture, described in Chapter 3, provided us with reference points to which data concerning change could be contrasted.

The *patrins* of scientific humanism guided us also to the study of individuals whose goals and levels of aspirations must somehow be accommodated within the cultural context. The nature of those goals and their realization is both product and process of the interaction of individual and culture. Hadley Cantril has concerned himself with this dynamic in his exploration of patterns of human concerns (1965) which suggested hypotheses and models helpful in identifying contemporary Gypsy expectations and wishes. Because by their very nature these data take introspective aspects of human behavior into account, the collection and analysis of Gypsy life histories were found to be essential to their development. Similarly, life history materials revealed the individual as creature, carrier, creator, and "manipulator" of his culture (Simmons 1967:388). Langness's work concerning the life history (1965), Hsu's guide to the study of literate societies (1969), and Goodman's discussion of cultural and individual autonomy (1967) were found to contain both suggestions and reinforcements concerning methodological and theoretical approaches. Where possible, verbatim translations of taped interviews are included in the text for, as Honigmann has noted, "motivation and culture are not isomorphic. Motives must be assessed through studying living individuals in depth" (1961:99).

The Unsolved X

Evolving out of shared concerns, anthropologists and psychologists are increasingly recognizing the need to test psychological theories transculturally, to study behavioral changes both as causes and effects of cultural change, and to refine the use of experimental design in nonlaboratory settings. While some notable efforts have been made to utilize psychological techniques in anthropological field research, in the main, these have been psychoanalytically oriented. There has been a growing awareness of the need to broaden the scope of interdisciplinary research in order to study human concerns in nonclinical as well as clinical situations. As noted by Cantril, it is essential that we study "both persons and People, both men and Man" (1965:29). Testing hypotheses derived from the study of the individual and, conversely, those derived from the study of societies, psychologists and anthropologists are in a position today to share mutually supportive methodologies and theories.

Thus, in this book, reflecting as it does the sharing of actual field experiences and interdisciplinary dialogues, we hope that we may come a bit closer to understanding that society which, as Linton has told us, is, in the last analysis, a group of individuals. "These individuals constitute an unsolved X in every cultural equation, and an X which cannot be solved by purely anthropological techniques" (1945:xv).

"In the shadow of the Alhambra"

Flood-damaged caves, Upper Region

1

The Gitanería

O city of the gypsies!
Who that has seen can forget?
Federico García Lorca

THE ANDALUSIAN GYPSY has been variously described as Spain's anti-hero, its provocation, its exaggeration. His foothold is rooted most firmly in southern Spain, in its harsh sun-baked soil, in its wild sierras. As durable as the olive trees whose gnarled trunks and branches appear to be forever frozen in a bitter yet humorous ballet, the Gypsy has survived and placed his stamp of individuality on Andalusian culture. His songs, his dances, his life style are blends of reality and fantasy, passion and shrewdness, joy and sadness. A living paradox, he has both enthralled and exasperated us in our work.

In his role of picaroon, the Gypsy is master of the arts of flattery and persuasion in the service of his own interests. His roguish sense of humor—"I sold one mule three times over at the fair last year for the fun of it"—occasions little resentment, even among its victims. Sought after at Spain's *ferias* (fairs) for his gifts of wit, cleverness, *gracia* (charm), he nevertheless remains true to his own elemental nature—brooding, restless, loyal, fiercely proud, and aloof. He delights in confusing us, a game by which he elevates and preserves his own sense of uniqueness. Knowing our secrets well, he reveals few of his own. When he does, his trust and love are absolute, factors which have delayed the writing of this book for years.

"I remember the night they brought you to me. We have been talking for eleven years." The old Gypsy chief, in failing health and wondering if he would survive the coming winter, recalled our first meeting. Inextricably linked with his love for Doña Rosario (the late Duchess of Lécera), whose death marked the passing of "better days," his reminiscences evoked images of Granada, the Sacro Monte, and Gypsy *zambras* of old.

We danced our *zambras* in the gardens of Doña Rosario's *carmen* [villa]. She was *muy flamenca* [gypsified, lively] and introduced us as her friends to Segovia, the Marquesa of this and that, Pastora Imperio—all. I would play the guitar and sing, and my wife, La Golondrina, would dance. Isabel and Maria too [his daughters]. In those gardens you know, on top of the city of Granada, we would dance all night long until morning. She never let us leave without breakfast. And she would bring her friends to our *cueva*, to our *fiestas*. Sometimes she came alone and ate *olla* with us. She cared much for us, and we loved her as a Gypsy.

6

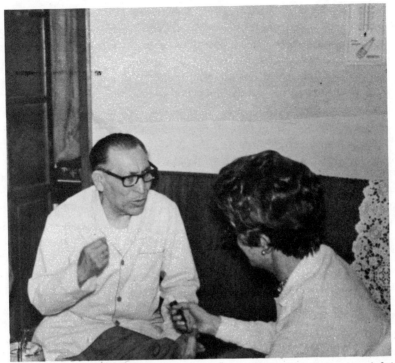

"We have been talking for eleven years." (Author Bertha Quintana, right)

The little villa today is a silent museum dedicated to Manuel de Falla, who wrote his *Nights in the Gardens of Spain* while in residence there. The Gypsies dancing in the moonlight are poorly recreated in nearby outdoor nightclubs whose slickness and impersonality bear no relationship to the private Gypsy *juergas* (revelries) of which Joaquín spoke. Attended by tourists, herded and prodded through their cultural paces by guides whose primary focus is the size of the evening's commission, the commercial *zambra* today lacks the intimacy and responsiveness needed to draw out the *duende* (demon, spirit, soul) of the Gypsy performer. Dependent upon a sense of spiritual communion between dancer, singer, guitarist, and aficionado, the *duende* cannot be conjured up so many times an evening at so many pesetas per inspiration. And yet, it may spring suddenly out of even the most listless and crass of performances.

Last summer we witnessed, as we have many times, a *zambra* performed in a Sacro Monte cave for a busload of Scandinavian tourists. Depicting a Gypsy wedding, the *gitanas*, some of them little more than children, moved in swirls of skirts, ruffles, and fringe through the various dance stages of "eyeing the bride," elopement, and fear of parental reprisal. Leading up to the celebrated *cachucha*, one of the few pure Gypsy dances still performed by them, the *gitanas* and a male dancer, accompanied by *cuadro* (flamenco performing team) singers, *jaleadores* (beat setters), and guitarists, enacted the stealing of the bride, the fear of the *novio* (bridegroom) in approaching her parents, and, finally, the pardon and tribal fiesta.

After drinking small glasses of *manzanilla,* the tourists left. Some of the performers left with them only to return shortly with hot baked potatoes wrapped in newspaper which they shared with us. The old chief, pressed into playing his guitar at a time in life when he should have been sitting in the sun, strummed it softly. His *duende,* as though lurking in the background to which his age entitled him, but denied him by his life circumstances, suddenly took over.

"I feel like singing a *siguiriya* (weeping song) for Berta," he announced abruptly. His age and poor health forgotten, his Great Song burst forth and beat against the walls of the small cave. What hidden memories of the past stirred him, or what precisely in eleven years of friendship had moved him to this passionate declaration of anguish and invincibility, we do not know. But, with his face contorted as though gripped by great pain, he sang "without throat" of despair, of hope, of the tragic sense of life which is the essence of Deep Song.

We were reminded of his early life when, as a child, he worked the bellows that kept the fires burning at the forges of his metalworking father; of his description of how the little fires would light the Granada night so that when one stood at the Alhambra looking over to the Sacro Monte and Albaicín (the old Moorish quarter), it looked as though the very earth glowed; of his first guitar, and of his grief that his father had not lived to see him play it well. His song reminded us of all of these things and of his devotion to his "woman," their life together; of their pride in the great *zambras* they had mounted in their *cuevas* (caves); of their shared worry that now the best of the dancers and singers were leaving the Sacro Monte so that old men and women had to work again. And, out of the dark depths of his *siguiriya,* we were somehow moved back in time to those nights when Joaquín and Doña Rosario had shared their common humanity in that garden on top of the city of Granada.

The city, for all of its expansion and tourism, had lost little of its *duende.* A legendary city, Granada is best described in terms of mood rather than in precise detail. Its Sacro Monte Gypsy quarter is an exaggeration of its surprising contrasts in which neither the past nor the present are clearly separable. The Sierra Nevada rings the city, and yet does not enclose it; the *vega* (great plain), stretching out below, holds its own against even the 10,000-foot snow-capped mountains which tower in the background. The delicacy of its Moorish heritage dominates the excesses of Baroque influences which, in turn, exist comfortably amid Roman, Gothic, and Renaissance buildings and relics.

Standing in somewhat uneasy juxtaposition to all of the visible reminders of Granada's nostalgic past are new apartment complexes which each year extend the lower city further out into the *vega.* A tropical city in summer, from which snow is visible on the mountaintops even in July, Granada's architecture, history, and climate are characterized by a diversity homogenized only in the delight of its people in art, music, conversation, and small elemental things. An intimate city, Granada's mystical mood provides the perfect setting for the perpetuation of its Gypsy quarter, from which the sounds of Gypsy music mingle at night with those of barking dogs, city traffic, and the movement of people in *paseo* (promenade).

However, the essence of Granada remains captured above all in the Alhambra, the red palace of its sultans, sitting as it does on the Sabika mountain, Granada's "crown." From its parapets the jumble of small white buildings and narrow streets of the Albaicín appear to tumble down into the Darro Gorge, only to rise sharply again to the Sacro Monte.

Approached by the narrow Camino del Darro, which takes its name from the river it borders, the Sacro Monte is entered through an open plaza faced with small shops. Its most famous caves are near the road, their whitewashed dazzle serving as background for the colorful array of the *gitanas*, who beckon visitors with sharp calls to their commercial *zambras*: "¡Mire el baile! ¡Qué gitano! ¡Mire, mire!" The staccato sounds of the dancers' heels, hand clapping, the despairing wail of a singer, and the tumultuous cries of Gypsies calling one to another are accentuated in the frantic competition for *zambra* clients. Like the polka-dotted dresses of the *gitanas* and the flamenco shirts of their male companions, the atmosphere is staged, the players changing into their costumes and taking their positions as visitors start arriving. The Gypsy has carefully studied what the *payo* (non-Gypsy) expects of him, and he plays his role to perfection.

The *zambras* of "La Golondrina" are held in three caves situated in this lower region. Copper pots, utensils, brasses of various shapes and sizes, and photographs of the great dancers and singers who have performed there, hang in glittering disarray from the walls and ceilings. Straight-backed chairs line the walls in hopeful expectation of the tourists who will pay to see the *cuadro* perform in the tiny floor space into which they will crowd. Worried over the shortage of performers and the falling off of *turismo* (tourism), Joaquín, his wife, and Isabel anxiously listen for the sounds of tour buses groaning up the Camino del Sacro Monte. Sharp commands keep the *gitanas* at readiness.

Beyond this public area, narrow, rocky passages rise steeply to the upper residential caves, which sit in ever ascending levels far above the tumult below. The atmosphere here is quiet, almost sleepy, the sounds of guitars and castanets giving way to the soft plodding of donkeys carrying milk cans on their door-to-door rounds, and to the laughter of small naked children playing in the dust. This is an arid land, broken by irregular paths leading to its public wells, and upper and lower regions.

The caves, which appear to be haphazardly carved out of the mountainside, vary in size and condition. Many, one-room homes, lack even a door. Whitewashed inside and out, their rough limestone walls protect their inhabitants from the heat of summer and the icy winds which blow down from the sierra in winter. Curtained entrances reveal the extreme poverty under which some Sacro Monte Gypsies continue to live. Lacking electricity, water, plumbing facilities of any kind, this type of cave was hardest hit by the floods of 1963, which ruined at least half of the upper caves of the poorer Gypsies. Declared uninhabitable by government decree, hundreds of Gypsies were forced out of them and into the *barrio* (district) known as La Chana.

Life in La Chana, which was to have been "temporary" according to government relocation policy, bears some similarity to the life style of the Sacro Monte. Like ghettos everywhere, however, La Chana is overcrowded, and the

Cante flamenco

Gypsy Zambra:
Cueva de la Golondrina

La cachuca

Fandango gitano

poverty of its people far more apparent than in the Sacro Monte. Large Gypsy families live in two or three rooms, row upon row of these temporary quarters spreading out over a flat and incredibly dusty area on the outskirts of Granada. Described as cold in winter and extremely hot in summer, only the colorful laundry, which seems to be draped everywhere, suggests the Gypsy of romantic literature.

Many of La Chana's Gypsy residents continue to engage in *zambra* activities and are transported back to the Sacro Monte daily. The caves utilized for performances were virtually untouched by the floods. Similarly, the more elaborate residential caves of the quarter remained intact. The latter reflect the relative affluence of their Gypsy owners. Facades have been added to many of these homes, which from a distance create the illusion of rather substantial structures. Providing in some instances one or even two extra rooms, they lead into the smaller and older *cuevas*.

One such complex consists of three units enclosing a shaded patio. In the largest, a salon/dining area is flanked by two small bedrooms, each of which contains a large brass bedstead. Electrified, neatly whitewashed, and immaculately clean, this unit is comfortably albeit not sumptuously furnished. In 1970, a television set, being paid for by so many *peseta*s a week, had replaced a refrigerator formerly located in a prominent place of honor in the living room. The refrigerator had finally been moved into a second cave, which housed the unit's kitchen. Everywhere the walls were decorated with gleaming copper utensils, miniature pots and pans, family photographs, religious scenes, and pictures of the Saints. Wrought iron and Alpujarra fabrics, together with straight-backed carved chairs, gave the main room its "Spanish feel," while a highly polished modern sideboard suggested Grand Rapids rather than Nasrid Granada. Meals were served at a small round table covered in checkered plastic. The pedestal of the table held a *brasero* (fire pan), which was filled with hot coals in winter; family members are warmed by sitting around the table, their legs covered by a floor-length tablecloth. Although designed for a maximum of four people, the table seemed capable of stretching (as did the food) to accommodate as many relatives and friends as chose to appear at mealtime. We counted twelve on one occasion, "a small group," our Gypsy host explained.

Forming the far wall of the patio was still another cave, the family bath equipped with tub, shower, wash basin and toilet. Partially tiled, this room was a source of great pride, and its hospitalities were urged upon us. The patio was hand scrubbed daily, as were all the rooms, and a wild profusion of potted plants lined its sides. Shade was provided by a carefully nurtured solitary lemon tree, and by grapevines strung between buildings.

A stairway leading to the roof of the facade served as both terrace and as the area from which the family wash hung in the sun. The Alhambra, the Generalife palace, and the old Alcazaba on top of the Albaicín towered above. From this vantage point, glimpses into lower caves enabled the family to keep track of relatives, visitors, and other neighbors.

In spite of the close intimacy of these cave dwellings, the fact that they face inward, their backs to the narrow footpaths servicing them, perpetuates a sense of privacy—the antithesis of the bedlam to which tourists are exposed below.

This is the true *gitanería* (Gypsy quarter) of Granada's Gypsies, the home toward which elder residents of La Chana continue to look, and to which its most celebrated artists traditionally returned. As noted by one Gypsy elder,

> We came to Granada with *los Reyes Católicos* [Ferdinand and Isabel] five-hundred years ago. Since then we have been here in the Sacro Monte and the Albaicín living and dying, like our parents before us, in the shade of the Alhambra.

Seeing advantage in keeping alive legends which attribute to their metal-working ancestors the forging of the projectiles used in the reconquest of Granada, Gypsies place themselves in the Royal Caravan which entered the city in 1492. Ironically, the end of Moorish rule in Spain also marked the end (for nearly three centuries to come) of the relatively carefree existence enjoyed by Gypsies in Andalusia. Ignoring the fact that Gypsy repression in Spain was first legalized by Ferdinand and Isabel, Granada's Gypsies deny their earlier association with Moorish rule.

Their survival dependent upon outwitting the *payo*, Gypsies use and romanticize those aspects of history which best serve their interests and needs. Questions about who they are and where they came from continue to be answered in the *gitanerías* of southern Spain by tales of "royal blood" and ancient Egyptian kingdoms. Reinforcing their pride and arrogance, these tales are used, more importantly, to protect and preserve their cultural aloofness. Choosing to remain on the fringes of civilization, Gypsies keep its imperfections at arm's length by shrouding themselves in a mysterious past. Residents of a dream city, Granada's Gypsies wear its mystical moods, like a *mantón* (shawl), "with style."

┌─────┐
│ 2 │
└─────┘

Gypsies in Andalusia

O' I am not of gentle clan
I'm sprung from Gypsy tree;
And I will be no gentleman,
But an Egyptian free.
Borrow 1908:297

What Is a Gypsy?

LOOKING BACK IN TIME, bands of Gypsies who invaded western Europe in 1417 (estimated to have numbered between 120 and 400 members) answered this question by pointing to Egypt as their homeland. In accounting for themselves, one of the most persistently cited claims attributed to these early nomads was the declaration that they were penitents, condemned to wander throughout the world for seven years because of a curse placed upon their Egyptian ancestors for having refused protection to the Holy Family from Herod. George Borrow, in 1841, described the similarities in this story to the fate foretold the ancient Egyptians in certain chapters of Ezekiel. Unable to accept the belief that the Gypsies invented the tale, and noting their lack of familiarity with Scripture, he believed that it

> ... probably originated amongst the priests and learned men of the east of Europe, who, startled by the sudden apparition of bands of people foreign in appearance and language, skilled in divination and the occult arts, endeavored to find in Scripture a clue to such a phenomenon ...

Borrow concluded that, although there were no means to ascertain whether the Gypsies believed from the first in this story,

> ... they most probably took it on credit, more especially as they could give no account of themselves. ... The tale moreover answered their purpose, as beneath the garb of penitence they could rob and cheat with impunity, for a time at least (1908:126–129).

Whatever the origin of the tale of Egyptian descent, it appears that the Gypsies found it to be in harmony with the times, so much so that, as Starkie has pointed out, the success of Gypsy penetration into fifteenth-century western Europe was due in part to the fact that they had arrived at a time when Christian pilgrimages to Rome and to Santiago de Compostela were at their height.

13

The Gypsies as pilgrims found, at first, open doors everywhere in Europe, because they were looked upon as sacred men and women who should be helped to accomplish their penance, for it was the duty of charitable Christians to speed on their way those undertaking the long journey to Compostela, and to give them all the assistance they needed (Starkie 1957:146).

In addition, indications are that the story told by the Gypsies of being kings, dukes, and earls of a kingdom known as Little Egypt, from whence they had been driven by conquering infidels, also served to engender a sympathetic response in their new audiences, as well as to enhance their status in general throughout Europe. Aside from the convincing manner of the Gypsies, the appearance, dress, and royal demeanor of their chiefs lent an air of authenticity to Gypsy assertions of royal origin. As visiting royalty, records show that the Gypsy chiefs were granted certain rights and privileges by the various European emperors and kings of the times, some of whom even guaranteed the Gypsies immunity from the laws of the very lands they penetrated. Among the privileges secured was the right to be tried only by Gypsy tribunals or, as in England, by a court composed half of Gypsies. They were given papal safe-conduct passes, money, and special permits to visit pilgrimage shrines throughout Europe. By municipal and royal decrees, local citizens of the areas visited by the Gypsies often were threatened with imprisonment and/or harsher punishments should they in any way injure them or refuse them alms. They enjoyed, too, the right granted only to kings and nobles of keeping hunting dogs to kill whatever game they came across.

In a lecture given at New York University in 1959, Starkie reported that in 1430 James V of Scotland went so far as to conclude a treaty with the Gypsy chief known as the Earl of Little Egypt in which the king pledged the support of his armies to help recover Little Egypt for the Gypsies. In other words, so convincing were the royal claims of the Gypsies that many of those occupying high royal and papal ranks with whom they established their first contacts did not bother to inquire even about the geographical location of Little Egypt. Starkie has called this "the first Great Trick (*Hokkano Baró*) they played upon the credulous *gorgios* (non-Gypsies) when they knocked at the gates of Europe" (1953:40).

While seldom disputed by the majority, there is some evidence to show that early Gypsy origin tales were occasionally questioned by individual observants during the fifteenth, sixteenth, and seventeenth centuries. By the latter part of the eighteenth and the early part of the nineteenth centuries, however, the Egyptian origin tale began to appear less and less frequently in accounts of them, being replaced increasingly by data which traced the Gypsies back to India rather than to Egypt. Outstanding among the scholars of this era, Grellman laid sound foundations for subsequent linguistic studies by his analysis of the Gypsy language, the so-called Romany tongue. He found that it was basically composed of Sanskrit words, many still in pure form, and that it most closely resembled the dialects spoken in northwestern India (1807:11–14). He concluded from his research that the Gypsies originated in India, a finding later confirmed not only by modern linguists but by anthropological studies of Gypsy physical characteristics as well. Referring to these, Kroeber noted that the Gypsies "originated in India, and they show definite evidence of that fact in their blood type and in the Romany speech of which they retain remnants, in addition to the language of whatever country they inhabit" (1948:279). More recently, in discussing reproductive isolation and the Gypsies of Europe, Hulse concluded, "The idea that their original home-land was India is supported by analysis of blood group frequencies as well as by observation of their external physical features. In both they resemble certain lower caste groups of northwestern India rather than the Europeans among whom they dwell" (1963:386–387).

Evidence of an Indian heritage was found also in studies of Gypsy music; Brown (1929:118–125), Falla (1950:127–130), and Starkie (1935:6–13) all drawing attention to its Indian characteristics. Among these, the falling cadence, the complicated arabesques, the infinite gradations of pitch, the repetition of the same note, the cultivation of metallic tone, and the multiplicity of conflicting rhythms, all were found to adhere more closely to those of Indian music than to any other.

While the preponderance of evidence pointing toward an Indian ancestry has been accepted by virtually all Gypsy scholars and anthropologists today, there remain countless numbers of Gypsies, particularly in southern Spain, who con-tinue to keep alive the tale of Egyptian origin. As a people who have kept no written records of their migrations, it would appear that of all the myths associated with their origin, the one which gave them their first status in western Europe is the one still favored by many Andalusian Gypsies. To the myths, however, must be added the reality of early migrations by some Gypsy nomads into Spain via Africa, involving movements through and from Egypt. "The Spaniards quickly gave them the name of 'Gitanos,' . . . and this time the nomads really had come from Egypt" (Clébert 1963:84). Whatever their reasons, even in 1970, Andalu-sian Gypsy entertainers continue to call themselves by such names as La Faraona (Pharaoh's daughter), and the word "Gypsy" itself, a derivation of the word "Egyptian," attests to the high degree of survival throughout the world of the old tales.

Movement into Spain

The Gypsies' fall from favor in central Europe, France, and Italy was not many years in coming, abusing as they did the rights and privileges accorded them by church and state. Not only did they prove themselves to be thoroughly irre-ligious, but also their considerable talents for bewitching local populaces with superstitions and a wide variety of occult claims readily brought them into open conflict with church officials (Starkie 1953:35–38).

Perhaps the most famous Gypsy method of duping those with whom they came in contact was the Hokkano Baró, or the Great Trick. As described by Borrow this consisted in

> persuading some credulous person to bury or otherwise hide his money, jewelry, or silver in a pre-determined spot for a pre-determined period of time. The Gypsy perpetrating this trick meanwhile had convinced his victim that the treasure would multiply itself provided that it was not looked upon or touched during

the stated time period, rarely less than three days. While the victim waited for the days to pass, not only had the Gypsy carried the treasure away, but also he had managed to place time and safe distance between himself and his victim. There were numerous subtle variations of the *Hokkano Baró*, but its essential elements remain as described (1908:256–259).

Furthermore, the beginnings of rumors of alleged Gypsy practices of child stealing, cannibalism, and witchcraft combined to close many doors heretofore open to them. Aside from these circumstances, however, an even more practical consideration was beginning to contribute to the growing European hostility toward them. By 1438 the ranks of what had started out as relatively small bands were being swelled continuously by thousands of Gypsies eager to share in the earlier success of their people (Starkie 1957:147). Still under orders in many areas to give them alms, shelter, and other forms of aid, the hardships suffered by hapless peasants and townsfolk attempting to cope with these new parasitic hoards moving into Europe became increasingly severe and numerous. All of these factors, as well as other excesses of which the Gypsies were guilty, hastened their excommunication by the clergy, on the one hand, and their banishment by state authorities, on the other, a major consequence of both acts being the mass movement of thousands of Gypsies into Barcelona by 1447. While the Gypsies were not complete strangers to Spain when they made their appearance in Barcelona (earlier movements into Spain and migrations from North Africa via Gibraltar having been recorded), it was not until the arrival of the second and larger wave of Gypsies that the Gypsy story in Spain really had its significant beginnings. There, capitalizing on the lack of communication facilities and political unrest, and using their talents for presenting themselves in a guileless light, once again Gypsies began to prosper as noble penitents from Little Egypt.

Social and Political Climate
of Fifteenth-Century Andalusia

The Spain into which thousands of Gypsies moved in the mid-fifteenth-century years was a land still divided, albeit the Granada coastal area of Andalusia was its only remaining Islamic stronghold. The Gypsies, moving in numerous small bands, and using Catalonia as their principal corridor, fanned out into all of Spain. They soon distinguished between those provinces most congenial to their way of life and those less suitable. They favored the provinces of Valencia, Estremadura, New Castile, and Murcia,

> . . . but, far, far more, Andalusia, . . . Andalusia, the land of the proud steed and the stubborn mule, the land of the savage sierra and the fruitful and cultivated plain: to Andalusia they hied, in bands of thirties and sixties; . . . (Borrow 1908:45).

With reference to early Gypsy settlements in southern Spain, the noted French gypsiologist Jean-Paul Clébert has called attention to the probable meeting there of "African" and "European" Gypsies.

We do not know the date on which the Gypsies crossed the Strait of Gibraltar. . . . Where and when did the meeting of the two groups take place? This also is not known. . . . Spanish documents never speak of two different groups of nomads. They simply mention *gitanos*. . . . We remember that the northern Gypsies arrived at Barcelona in 1447. . . . The arrival of the southern *gitanos* could only have happened earlier. The *gitanerías* or *gitano* colonies in the south of the peninsula seem to have been established at an earlier date than those of the north: the Sierra Nevada mountains must have given shelter to the first tribes, and the *gitano* colonies of Andalusia at Granada, Cadiz and Seville have been attested "at all times" (1963:85).

When and however these meetings occurred, the Gypsies in Spain principally identified themselves with Andalusia, an area where, from all historical accounts, they found that the harsher elements of life had been softened by the preoccupation of its people with the arts, romanticism, and oriental mysticism. This seemed to be especially the case in Nasrid Granada, for it was within this legendary kingdom of the Moors that the Gypsies concentrated in the greatest numbers. Here, the cultures of the Moors, the Jews, and the Spaniards had amalgamated to produce a standard of living marked by a philosophic fatalism which the Gypsies found to be particularly congenial to their own traditions. And, here, in what has since come to be regarded as the well-spring of Spanish Gypsy culture, the *gitanos*, some settling in the caves of the Sacro Monte, and others maintaining their nomadic existence, successfully and with relative impunity, continued to ply their trades of metalworking, mule clipping, horse trading, minstrelry, and fortune-telling.

The political climate of Andalusia, however, was something far less perfect than its topographical and socioeconomic features. Torn for decades by protracted power contests, the Islamic kingdom of Granada was beginning to hear the sounds of its own death rattle. Violating in 1466 the truce established with Christian Spain, the terms of which stated that an annual tribute of gold was to be paid to the Spanish sovereigns out of Granada's treasury, Muley Abul Hacen, Granada's ruler from 1466 to 1488, attempted to reestablish his kingdom's complete autonomy (Harrison 1903:210–211). The stormy union of Spain, finally accomplished under the joint rule of Ferdinand and Isabel, threats of war with Portugal, and the need of the Spanish crown to strengthen its own instruments of internal control all operated to forestall open hostilities with the Muslim stronghold until 1479. In that year, only two months after making peace with Portugal, Isabel petitioned the pope for crusading privileges aimed at the reconquest of Granada. The delayed Spanish answer to Abul Hacen's refusal to meet Ferdinand's demand for payment of the annual tribute was to prepare for the campaign which ultimately ended Islamic rule in western Europe.

The bloody struggle for the Nasrid kingdom, consisting as it did of fourteen cities, ninety-seven fortified palaces, and many formidable castles, began in earnest in 1481, following a sudden attack by the Muslims against the Christian fortress of Zahara. Aided by internal Muslim rivalries and, finally, by civil war in Granada, the Catholic sovereigns made steady progress against their enemy. Taking one city at a time, by 1491, only one, Granada, the beautiful and peerless pride of the Moors, now cut off from all outside sources of supply, remained to be conquered. Establishing their camp outside the city walls in what, today, is Santa Fe, Ferdinand and Isabel chose to sit out their last siege, waiting for the formal capitulation of the destitute and torn city. Long months of hunger, internal political strife, and the continual defeats suffered by the Muslims in all of their last attempts to cut through the Chrisian lines culminated in January 1492, when the keys to the Alhambra were finally delivered up by Boabdil, the last Islamic king of Granada, to the waiting Ferdinand and Isabel. "Boabdil's words at this historic moment are different in every source, but those recorded by Fernandez de Oviedo, who was present, are as simple and touching as any: 'My Lord, these are the keys to your Alhambra and your city; Go, Sire, to possess them.' The king handed the keys to Isabel. . . ." (Miller 1964:135).

During the ten years of war the Gypsies in Andalusia seem to have prospered in some areas by supporting the Catholic cause and in others by aiding the Muslims. The record of the role played by the Gypsies during the hostilities is fragmentized, however, and seems to be based more on inference than on verifiable facts. Tradition has held that the Gypsy metalworkers who established themselves outside the walls of Granada in the caves of the Sacro Monte forged the projectiles used by Ferdinand and Isabel to defeat attempts by the Muslims to end the Spanish siege (Ortiz de Villajos 1949:27). Bercovici maintained that the Gypsies "preferred serving as spies for the Moors against the Spaniards to serving the Spaniards against the Moors" (1928:152). Borrow's answer to the question was, "the *gitanos*, who cared probably as little for one nation as the other, . . . doubltess sided with either as their interests dictated, officiating as spies for both parties and betraying both" (1908:83).

Whatever the right answer, it seems doubtful that the question is of major importance other than to illustrate the fact that the Gypsies participated, by their presence, at least, in this crucial period of Spanish history. Based on the fact that the first and deepest loyalty of the Gypsy is to his own people, a theme which will be developed in a later chapter, and considering, too, the traditional aversion of Gypsies to military service, their role in the reconquest of Granada was probably no more than a minor one, little affecting the war's final outcome one way or the other. Of great importance, however, was the affect of the postwar years on the subsequent position to be occupied by the Gypsies in Andalusian culture.

The Gypsy in Spanish Law

Seven years after the reconquest of Granada, the Gypsies' position in Spanish society began to assume a new character which was to stand in sharp contrast to the relatively unmolested and carefree existence they had enjoyed during their early years on Spanish soil. Nowhere is this fact made more evident than in Spanish law, the principal instrument of control employed for three centuries to effect either the total assimilation or the extinction of the Gypsies in Spain. A backward look at the Gypsy record as reflected in Spanish law has served Gypsy historians both by clarifying the role played by the law in the adaptive process and by underlining certain characteristics of Gypsy culture which persist today.

In spite of the fact that many of the laws against the Gypsies were framed during the same period that the Spanish Inquisition was systematically operating to destroy all vestiges of Muslim, Jewish, and Protestant influence in Spain, the Gypsies, notorious for their contempt of religious observances, were never persecuted on that score. Borrow has reported that the Inquisition looked upon the Gypsies with such contempt that "it was a matter of perfect indifference to the holy office whether they lived without religion or not, . . . the *gitanos* having at all times been *gente barata y despreciable* [low and contemptible people]" (1908:134). He went on to develop his theory that had the Gypsies been learned or wealthy enough to pose a threat to the ambitions of either the church or state, they too would have been consumed by the flames of the faggot piles. Starkie has carried this theme even further by presenting evidence to show that "it was, indeed, *due* to the Inquisition that the Gypsies were not victims of far greater persecution in Spain" (1953:45). Escaping, then, the long arm of the Inquisition, the persecution of the Gypsies in Spain was dominated primarily by the felt need to control their growing numbers, their nomadic tendencies, and their frequently dishonest methods of gaining a livelihood.

The legal record of Gypsy persecution had its beginnings in 1499, when Ferdinand and Isabel issued a pragmatic sanction at Medina del Campo demanding that the Gypsies abandon within sixty days their wandering throughout the kingdom and settle in one place under "masters" governing their employment or be exiled for life. The monarchs provided in their law for even harsher punishments, including slavery, for all Gypsies caught violating its terms more than once. In 1539, during the reign of Charles V (I of Spain) and Juana, the edict of Medina del Campo was compounded by the addition of a clause condemning male Gypsies between the ages of twenty and fifty to the galleys for six years prior to permanent exile should they be caught wandering anywhere in Spain (Borrow 1908:154–156). Other laws, including one which forbade them to trade or sell unless they had notarized proof of a settled residence, showed a marked tendency toward increasing severity, until by 1619, Philip III was found asserting that the Gypsies were not a "nation" but rather "a collection of vicious people drawn from the dregs of Spanish society" (Starkie 1953:48). This assertion appeared the same year as the celebrated discourses of Sancho de Moncada, Professor of Holy Scripture at the University of Toledo, which included the proposal that the Gypsies be condemned to death as Spanish vagrants. On the basis of his belief, Philip III forbade the Gypsies, again under the threat of exile, to use the name, dress, and language of the Gypsies "in order that, . . . this name and manner of life may be evermore confounded and forgotten" (Borrow 1908:135–157). In declaring the Gypsies not to be Gypsies but Spaniards, Philip III placed himself in the curious position of implying that his own subjects were not his responsibility but, rather, that upon failure to comply with his orders they became the rightful responsibility of the reigning monarch of some unidentified country. The fact was, however, that even had the Gypsies been desirous of leaving the Iberian Peninsula, anti-Gypsy laws passed in France, Germany, and Italy would have operated to discourage their recrossing the Pyrenees and retracing their old European steps. Again in 1633 Philip IV reiterated the charge that the Gypsies were actually useless Spaniards, and he demanded that all Gypsy colonies be broken up and that further intermarriage between those who called themselves Gypsies be prohibited. This attempt at total assimilation failing, still more restrictive laws were passed by Philip IV and Philip V until by 1783 the Gypsies were forbidden to ply any of their traditional trades, keep or use horses or mares, leave their places of domicile, or even take refuge in the churches. (For a detailed account of these laws, reference is directed toward the previously quoted works of Borrow and Starkie.)

Perhaps no better testimony to the overall ineffectiveness of these laws is the number and the severity of the laws themselves. Between 1499 and 1783 Spain's monarchs issued and revised during each of their respective reigns at least twelve anti-Gypsy laws, each one more strongly worded than the last. And, as all the laws failed in their stated purposes, it is not surprising that the reasons given for justifying their increasing severity took on more ominous overtones as the years passed. During the seventeenth and eighteenth centuries practically every crime in Spain was being laid at Gypsy feet. Starkie, in commenting upon this circumstance, has pointed out that the Gypsy did not create the Spanish underworld, but rather, finding in it elements that suited his mode of life, he gave to it semblances of tribal organization. He goes on to state that the most monstrous accusations against the Gypsies, including charges that they were experts in black magic and members of a sect in league with Satan, were the exaggerated products of the morbid imaginations of fanatics.

> In reality, the crimes of the Gypsies were of the petty kind that are called by professional criminals *descuido*, that is to say, indirect robbery. The Gypsy steals, but always without risking his own skin. If he is successful, his horses will feed and he pitches his tent; if he is found out he disappears, for he stalks his prey with great caution (1953:46–47).

One writer has attributed crimes of the Gypsies which were of a more violent nature to the fact that all of the Spanish laws of which the Gypsies were the object "provided the manner in which they should die, but not a single one the manner in which they might live" (Bercovici 1928:155). As a result, it has been concluded that the laws of the Spanish kings drove the Gypsies to reinforce their own laws in which hatred of all non-Gypsies predominated, and which served only to increase and extend their lawless state.

No Gypsy historian has ever failed to express surprise over the fact that, hunted as they were, Gypsies not only were able to survive and thrive in Spain but also concentrated in great numbers there.

> The Peninsula acts as a sounding board for Oriental races who usually give their richest sounds in it: the Arab, the Jew, and the Gypsy. It was in Spain that Arab civilization rose to its highest brilliancy; Spanish Jews were the greatest luminaries of Hebrew civilization since Biblical times; and as for the Gypsy, the superiority of the Spanish type over any other is not to be proved by books, but by the observation of the living specimens which may be found in Andalusia (Madariaga 1958:18).

No one single factor, however, has been held to account for this paradoxical twist of fate. Borrow tried to explain it principally in terms of the corruption of Spanish justice which enabled the Gypsies and their powerful friends to bribe local functionaries entrusted with administering the law (1908:152–154). Bercovici, too, stressed the fact that the Gypsies had introduced themselves into the homes of prominent Spaniards, providing them with diversions which, presumably, helped insure the Gypsies' prosperity and survival (1928:152). A law of Philip IV takes cognizance of these circumstances by providing for heavy fines in the case of the nobles, or ten years in the galleys in the case of plebeians, as punishment for aiding or abetting the Gypsies (Borrow 1908:161–162). (As the administration of this law was placed in the hands of the very people for whom it was intended, its success was no greater than that of any of its predecessors.)

All writers have emphasized the role which Spain's topography played in providing the Gypsies with ample wilderness in which to hide safely from their oppressors whenever the need arose. Starkie applied to the Gypsies the old Spanish proverb *"se obedece pero no se cumple* [we obey but do not comply]" in his explanation of the failure of Spanish law to assimilate them (1953:49). Throughout the long history of sixteenth-, seventeenth-, and eighteenth-century law in Spain, it appears that the Gypsies' response to all laws directed at their control was marked by characteristic indifference or, at best, by short-lived, superficial adaptation to their conditions; the need to outwit the hunter becoming no more nor less that part and parcel of the whole round of Gypsy life. Cut off, then, from other European countries which had legislated against them, protected by influential friends and the bribable state of Spanish justice, sheltered by wild terrain, and developing to the highest degree their own capacity for resistance, the Gypsy had yet to be tamed or made captive by Spanish law.

Such was the state of affairs in 1783, when the oft-quoted law of Charles III brought to a culmination centuries of legislation against the Gypsies. It was similar to former laws in that it stated that the Gypsies were not Gypsies by origin, that they were to give up their language, dress, and wanderings, and that

Nomadic Gypsies

punishment was to be inflicted upon all those resisting the law. However, the new law differed from its predecessors in that it prohibited but few types of employment to the Gypsy, stressing throughout that no distinction was to be made between those Gypsies who had renounced their Gypsy ways and other vassals of the state. The law forbade all Spaniards to address them as *gitanos*, and even provided for a system of fines to be levied against any who refused admission of "this class of reclaimed people" to their trades and guilds (Borrow 1908:166–173).

While lacking in many respects, particularly in its failure to take into consideration Gypsy traditions, the law of Charles III was noteworthy in that it gave the Gypsy the right to select his own occupation and to participate in community activities. The movement of the Gypsies into the towns of Andalusia, with its accompanying development and expansion of permanent settlements proved to be a gradual one. It was simultaneously accelerated by the catalytic effect of the law of Charles III, and delayed by the reluctance of the Gypsies to give up their nomadic existence for a sedentary one. Hesitantly and slowly, the Gypsy sedentary populations grew in proportion to the receptivity of the Andalusians toward them, and to the degree of opportunity open to the Gypsies in the towns (Starkie 1953:111). By the last half of the nineteenth century, however, they had become relatively stabilized, occasioning, through frequent culture contacts with Andalusians, the preoccupation with all things Gypsy which was to be felt throughout Spain.

Early Gypsy Culture Contacts in Andalusia

It has been said that art and life are one in Andalusia. While the Gypsy did not create this pattern, he was part of the fabric out of which the actual garment was cut. At no time in the history of Andalusia is this more apparent than during the latter half of the nineteenth century, when Andalusian accents illuminated the entire Spanish scene. What Ortega y Gasset has called the "dominating influence of Andalusia" (1937:88) in nineteenth-century Spain accounted in large measure for the fact that not only in Andalusia but throughout all of Spain as well, the accommodation process as related to the Gypsy was greatly accelerated and humanized during this period. Continuing into the twentieth century, until driven into obscurity by the chaos of the Spanish Civil War (1936–1939), Gypsy ascendancy in Spain was found to have paralleled closely developments in both artistic and intellectual circles.

Although culture contacts with the Gypsies had been ongoing in Andalusia since their first appearance there, the Gypsies having been engaged, for example, by Granada's city councils since the seventeenth century for the traditional dances in the annual Corpus Christi processions, it was not until the formation of what came to be known as the flamenco "caste" in the nineteenth century that the full impact of the *gitano* style was felt in Andalusian culture. Whatever its origin or original meaning, the word "flamenco" came to mean "Gypsy," and the class of Spaniards who associated with Gypsies or led a Gypsy-like life (Brown 1929: 21). It was applied, essentially, to the Gypsy personality as it reflected itself in

Andalusian culture, and to the music, not necessarily of Gypsy origin, of those who imitated Gypsy manners. Likewise, it was used to describe certain acts or things, especially those characterized by strong animation or wit. As described by Starkie, the constituency of the flamenco caste was Gypsies and Andalusian aficionados of the flamenco arts of music, dancing, and bullfighting. Its expansion was especially noticeable following the 1876 production of Bizet's opera *Carmen*, which, at that time, helped to make gypsified fashions the rage in Spain (1953:93).

Growing out of a long-standing pattern of accommodation, then, the formation and development of the flamenco caste served to facilitate and accelerate the process of Gypsy and Andalusian acculturation. Frequent meetings in the cafes, in the Gypsy quarters, and in the bullring brought into sharper focus personality characteristics which *gitanos* and Andalusians share in common. Starkie, in pursuing this theme, has drawn attention to the fact that both groups were made up of proud people with immense regard for tradition. Preoccupation with the death theme was characteristic also of both. He has noted further that the melancholy of the Andalusian was accentuated by the Gypsy, whom, the Andalusian said, *"tiene la alegría de estar triste* [rejoices in being sad]" (1953:96). That the Andalusian and the Gypsy recognized and understood this paradox of joy and sadness in one another has been advanced as one of the strongest arguments each had for accepting the other. In addition, both peoples placed a high value on individualism, as well as on familial loyalty.

Walter F. Starkie

Ortega y Gasset's analysis of Andalusian culture based upon its most misunderstood and elusive characteristic, its indolence, drew attention to the fact that by replacing maximum effort with minimum effort in establishing his ideal of life, the Andalusian [and the Gypsy] freed himself to enjoy a repertory of small and elemental delights (1937:96–99). These basic similarities, then, especially when coupled with the long histories of both Andalusians and Gypsies in dealing with diverse cultures, all tended to foster cultural exchanges between them.

Aside from the recognition of basic similarities in their respective cultures, the growth of empathy between these peoples has been traced also to the fact that the Andalusian found a quality to admire in the Gypsy's ability to imitate and perpetuate traditional folk arts and customs. For example, once the Gypsy was permitted to move into the professional ranks of the bullfighting art, frequently he came to excel the very Andalusian whom he imitated. Rather than occasioning resentment in a land where the bullfight was venerated, the Gypsy's facility in the bullring engendered a highly favorable and emotionally charged response in his Andalusian audiences. Starkie, in his review of this phenomenon as seen during the early part of the twentieth century, wrote,

> The Romanichals, indeed, evolved a definite Gypsy style of bullfighting, and certain chosen types among them won triumphs among the gentiles, such as, for example, the younger brother of Rafael el Gallo, known to all the world by the affectionate diminutive Joselito, who was acknowledged in our days to be supreme master, the inheritor of all great bullfighters (1953:112).

Ellis, too, joined the ranks of those who stressed the artistic affinity between the Gypsy and the Andalusian. Focusing his attention on the role of the Gypsy in Andalusian dancing, he concluded that

> it is in Spain, where the *gitano* has seized on the ancient Spanish dances with such zeal, and danced them with such fire and success, though sometimes with a touch of caricature, that many people have come to think that the dances are not Spanish at all but gypsy. . . . The gypsy has been attracted by certain congenial manifestations in the life of a nation, mastered them and specialized them, and so become on that side an appreciated element in the life of the people (1926: 175–176).

In addition, and of greatest importance, was the exchange which took place between the Gypsies and the Andalusians in their music. Brown has pointed out that the appreciation of the Andalusians for Gypsy music, and for the Gypsy's musical ability, which enabled him to adapt and preserve Spanish folk music much in the same way that he preserved their folk dances, resulted in the "blending" of many songs to a point where it became impossible to determine whether they were Andalusian or Gypsy in origin (1929:19). Similarly, the receptive milieu of Andalusia encouraged the Gypsies to preserve and perfect their own folk songs. Growing out of the Andalusian enthusiasm for the Gypsy style, the late-nineteenth- and early-twentieth-century years witnessed a phenomenal rise in Gypsy popularity in the world of professional entertainment, La Niña de los Peines, Pastora Imperio, La Macarrona, Manuel Torres, Manuel Centeno, Rita Ortega, Manuel Pavón, La Golondrina, La Jardín, Chacón, and Carmen Amaya being but a few of the outstanding Gypsy singers, dancers, and "stylists" whose names became known throughout Spain.

Even louder, however, and with more lasting effect, the echo of Gypsy music reached the ears of some of the world's greatest composers, many of whom incorporated the Gypsy idiom into what were to become celebrated classical works. Enrique Granados, Isaac Albéniz, Manuel de Falla, Turina, Spanish musicians who found inspiration in the oral and musical traditions of the Gypsies, were joined by Rimsky-Korsakov, Raoul Laparra, Glinka, Ravel, Claude Debussy, and Georges Bizet in drawing international attention to them (Trend 1929:15–35). The Deep Song Festival of 1922 also served to arouse enthusiasm, not only in Spain but in the outside world as well, for the strength and vitality of the musical heritage of Andalusia, which the Gypsies helped to create and perpetuate. Organized as a contest, the festival was held near the Alhambra where, to quote Brown,

> One of the most interesting parts of the fiesta was the vision of the band of Gypsies dancing in the courtyard of the Alhambra by moonlight. It was a symbol of the past and future of Andalusian folk art. During several centuries no one appreciated the beauty of the old Moorish palace, but the Gypsies who formerly lived in its halls unconsciously protected it from vandalism until the time came when all men could enjoy it. Thus it is with "deep song" and *baile gitano*: the Romanies have done much to preserve and perfect it; and now, as with the Alhambra, the time has come when all may enjoy its beauty (1929:150).

The Gypsy influence was reflected also in the works of artists of the period, including Zuloaga, Romero De Torres, and Augustus John—the last, eventually, to become a president of the Gypsy Lore Society (1937–1961). In the literature of Spain, too, the Gypsies came to occupy a prominent place; Federico García Lorca, Manuel Machado, and Juan Ramón Jiménez, the last a Nobel Prize winner in literature, being but a few of the celebrated writers of the period who, like Cervantes three hundred years earlier, drew inspiration from them. The fundamental themes of Gypsy culture served particularly to form the basis for major works of García Lorca, who, in his *Romancero Gitano* (*Gypsy Ballads*) and in his *Poema del Cante Jondo* (*Poem of Deep Song*), immortalized them. L. R. Lind, in his introduction to the Humphries' translation of the *Gypsy Ballads*, summed up their essence with the following statement:

> Through the Spanish gypsy, often more Spanish than the Spanish themselves, García Lorca describes, now with dry precise detail, again with sensuous images dazzling in their impact, the existence of the hunted outcasts of Spain, in whom the soul of the land bleeds and dies and renews itself, proud but flexible, rising in its bitter humor and ancient endurance against the oppression and cruelty of centuries (1954:52).

Significantly, all of the trends noted evinced a two-way acculturative exchange, the status of the Gypsy prior to the Spanish Civil War reflecting as much his willingness to participate in new (for him at least) aspects of Andalusian culture as it did the Andalusian's willingness to accept the Gypsy. Gradually, the Gypsy relinquished many practices which, in the past, had operated to keep him feared and segregated. He replaced them with new ways of earning a livelihood which, in general, were socially and legally sanctioned, all the while, however, holding fast to the most basic of his traditional beliefs and attitudes.

An opportunist always, the Gypsy selected and integrated into his own culture those traits of Andalusian culture which best suited his changing needs and wants. He did this in a manner designed both to produce the least chaos in Gypsy culture and to maintain its definite distinctness. He successfully resisted attempts at total assimilation. He was influenced by the people around him and, in turn, influenced them—but he remained uniquely "Gypsy."

Kroeber, in commenting upon phenomena of this nature, states that "since acculturation basically is the acceptance or borrowing of material from one culture by another, it always involves some approximation between the two cultures. But there is no reason why such approximation should continue into assimilation" (1948:428). In referring specifically to the Gypsies, he observes that "their distinctness lies above all in an attitude, or orientation, which leads them to select a certain group of activities in Western civilization and to discard most of the others. . . . They certainly have an ethos all their own" (1948:279).

The Gypsy Ethos

The ethos of Andalusian Gypsy culture as seen by a succession of Gypsy scholars, historians, and aficionados during the past century was dominated by extreme conservatism which had as its aim the preservation of fundamental Gypsy traditions. Paradoxically, foremost among the traditions which this conservatism sought to protect was the Gypsy ideal of freedom which, in itself, appeared to be the very antithesis of its controlling force. Characterized primarily by a passionate regard for everything *gitano*, Gypsy conservatism manifested itself in the norms, goals, and ethnocentric beliefs which were transmitted within the culture. Because "events happen repeatedly 'as in the *coplas*'" (Brown 1929:49), Gypsy culture has stressed endurance and preservation of the old mores and was uniquely resistant to external pressures.

In developing his well-known folk society concept, Redfield placed Gypsies at a midpoint between tribal and urban peoples, designating them as "transplanted folk" in whose society a significant number of elements were found to correspond to those he held to be characteristic of the "ideal" folk type. Field studies conducted in southern Spain during the first half of this decade revealed that the conventional ways of living of the Andalusian Gypsies, even though they had been influenced by those of non-Gypsy city populations, continued to bear a strong resemblance to elements found in Redfield's ideal construct. The all-pervading conservatism to which reference already has been made is a case in point, closely approximating, as it does, Redfield's observation that within the folk society there is little disposition to reflect upon traditional acts and consider them objectively or critically. Within the Gypsy system of tradition-oriented behavior it was noted that deeply emotional overtones colored the goals set by Andalusian Gypsies and that, in circular fashion, the goals were centered on the maintenance of the very traditions which gave rise to them in the first place. Redfield similarly drew attention to the fact that the goals found within folk societies were largely determined by custom, with great meaning attached to all individual endeavors made in directions indicated by tradition (1947:299–302).

In addition to these folk characteristics, a strong sense of "belonging together" manifested itself among Andalusian Gypsies in a pronounced personalized type of responsiveness to one another, and in extreme forms of cultural and biological ethnocentrism which were supported and reinforced by Gypsy law, origin tales, and folk arts. Extending kinship feelings outward into the society as a whole, inherent in the behavior of Gypsies was the assumption that feelings, interests, loyalties, and sentiments were shared, both in degree and kind, by all members of their group. These included the responsibility both to "share the good" as well as to avenge individual wrongs and injuries. Even among sedentary Gypsies, among whom there appeared to be a marked modern tendency toward relying upon local justice, a highly personalized type of identification with wronged members of their society was evident. This is not, however, to suggest that interpersonal relationships in Andalusian Gypsy culture were wholly harmonious, nor even dominantly so. Intragroup feuding, jealousies, and disagreements were observed to permeate the Gypsy life style, albeit their expression and resolution also tended to be regularized by tradition. The constraining nature of Gypsy law, to which further references will be made, and the Gypsy respect for tribal justice, with banishment the most dreaded punishment, operated to protect group welfare from both external and internal threat.

Dependent upon oral tradition, communication patterns in Gypsy culture were characterized by intimacy and a highly personalized intensity. The perpetuation of tradition was accorded full and sustained priority. The accommodation to Andalusian culture notwithstanding, Gypsy culture was found to be cohesive, distinctive, and deeply internalized by its participants. Its ethos remained "their own."

3

Themes in Traditional
Gypsy Culture

TO IDENTIFY THE TRADITIONAL THEMES the Andalusian Gypsies seek to transmit and perpetuate, data illustrative of the general character of their culture were examined first. Diaries, correspondence, memoirs, case histories, legal records, anthropological studies, biographies, folklore, histories of the Gypsies, literary sources, and published reports of missionaries, travelers, and others were utilized in this preliminary stage. Certain themes appeared to demonstrate how the Andalusian Gypsies viewed themselves as compared to others, and to find recurrent expression in Gypsy activities, attitudes, and artifacts as reported in these sources. These emergent themes were examined for frequency of expression, duration of existence, and preservation of characteristic unity, despite change. Themes found to have been maintained in Gypsy culture for more than three generations were provisionally designated as *traditional* themes. Those so designated were then validated in the field. The term "validation," as used in this context, refers to the identification of the posited themes in contemporary Gypsy culture through direct observation and field interviews.

Traditional cultural themes of the Andalusian Gypsies, as validated in field interviews conducted in southern Spain in 1959, included the following: (1) ethnic superiority (Gypsy pride), (2) preeminence of Gypsy law, (3) loyalty, (4) freedom, and (5) fatalism. Of the forty adult informants used in this phase of the first study, thirty were Andalusian Gypsies, and ten were non-Gypsies. The latter group consisted of authorities on Andalusian Gypsy culture, including scholars, artists, and aficionados recognized for their close, prolonged, and significant contacts with Gypsies. Both groups had an even distribution of adult male and female respondents.

In six subsequent field trips centering principally in Granada, we have had opportunity to both revalidate the themes and study their change and modification. Our deepening involvement in Gypsy life has had the effect of both sharpening and adding to our data. Working in an atmosphere of mutual trust which can develop only through time, we have been able to observe how the themes of Gypsy culture color and shape individual lives. We have added significantly over the years to the original sample. Gypsy and non-Gypsy adult informants unknown to us in 1959, Gypsy children, and public and private officials have more than tripled its size in the decade since past.

As has been noted, themes include unstated, covert aspects of culture that must be abstracted from the overt behaviors, attitudes, activities, and artifacts present. Yet not all themes are hidden, latent, or unverbalized. On the contrary, many are well known and made explicit by their practitioners in conversation, literature (oral or written), songs, and so forth. However, because the thematic content of culture tends to be highly internalized, that is, to be acted upon unconsciously, themes are seldom *readily* verbalized by participants in the culture. For example, the subtleties involved in the old Spanish proverb *"se obedece pero no se cumple"* (we obey but do not comply) may be illustrative of the fact that Gypsy law continues to exert a far more powerful influence over Gypsies in Andalusia than overt indications commonly would lead one to believe. Still, it is unlikely that Gypsy informants would make this distinction. The response "It is our way" may be as specific an answer as the field investigator will get. Consequently, dealing with culture themes requires, aside from sensitivity, that the investigator exercise extreme caution in abstracting them from cultural materials, and that he pay scrupulous attention to their treatment. Relative to this last point, Keesing noted "The fact that . . . the margin of subjectivity is likely to be great, and (we may add) methods are still crude and experimental, cannot deter efforts to formulate these great regularities in behavior and motivation" (1959:160).

A similar attempt at encapsulating cultural meaning and form is reflected in Hoebel's concept of *postulates* in culture, recently utilized by Hsu in his study of literate civilizations (1969:61–83). These focal points in the overall cultural integration in each society may serve as points of reference for compartive studies. In addition, they provide us with broadly generalized propositions "as to the nature of things . . . and as to what is qualitatively desirable and undesirable" (Hoebel 1954:13–14).

The enduring nature of the cultural themes discussed in this chapter is attested to by the fact that they may be identified even in the earliest literary references to Gypsy culture and that, as recently as in our 1970 study, they continue to manifest themselves in Gypsy life. No traditional culture themes in addition to those listed emerged from six subsequent field trips. Each theme is treated separately in the sections that follow, utilizing data from a variety of sources, including the most recent. Instead of ranking them in order of importance, the presentation of the themes has been designed to facilitate understanding of the way in which they support one another, and to reveal their overlapping nature.

Gypsy Pride

Don't speak wrongly of Gypsies
Who have the blood of kings
In the palms of their hands.
Cimorra 1943:184

The belief of Andalusian Gypsies in their ethnic superiority to non-Gypsies is reflected in virtually all Gypsy self-conceptions encompassing physical, cultural, and intellectual attributes. "As the Jews have the word *goi*, the Gypsies have *gadjo* [*payo* in southern Spain] . . . which means 'peasant,' 'countryman,' 'serf,'

La Golondrina:
Gypsy pride

which suffices to stress the sedentary 'clodhopper' aspect which they denigrate in us" (Clébert 1963:47). Even in relatively early studies, there is a high frequency of allusion to the proud mien of the Gypsies and to Gypsy vanity concerning their health and appearance. More than a century ago one investigator reported, "They have . . . an enormous share of vanity, which is evidenced in their fondness for fine clothes, and their gait and deportment when dressed in them" (Grellmann 1807:90). Similarly, contemporary observers of Granada's Gypsy population rarely fail to comment upon the hauteur of Gypsy demeanor—the high carriage of the head, the straightness of the back, the lift of the shoulders, the arrogant stride, the proud and penetrating Gypsy "gaze"—attributes which have contributed to the widespread and generally accurate feeling among non-Gypsies that they are disdainfully regarded by them.

Recently, in speaking of her wedding thirty years ago, a *gitana* of Granada described herself in these terms: "They made me a satin dress, and I wore a black mantilla, silver earrings, and a topaz cross—very pretty. I was sixteen years old and looked *muy guapa* [very handsome], even more *guapa* than I am now. My husband looked very handsome too, wearing a new suit—navy blue—and his *mosca* [mustache]. We looked *muy flamenco* [very lively] and so young—so young—that people gathered just to see us, and cried, 'How handsome are the two!'"

In spite of its strong cultural reinforcement, however, Gypsy vanity is not totally unfounded in physical fact. The early environmental stresses of the Gypsy life style undoubtedly contributed toward the maintenance of a high level of physical stamina among them, with only the strongest surviving its rigors. Physical and social selection for the harshness of nomadic life has been cited by many investigators as the main reason why the physical vigor and health of the Gypsies has always tended to be good, and why the proportion of seriously physically or mentally handicapped has always been low among them. In addition, and perhaps more significantly, extreme forms of cultural and biological endogamy have operated to preserve certain genetic distinctions among Gypsies even in modern times.

Of the anthropologists, Kroeber noted,

> It is customary, but mainly inaccurate, to speak of . . . the Gypsy race. . . . The Gypsies are a self-constituted caste, with folkways, occupations, and at least Romany speech remnants of their own. They have mostly preserved their dark Mediterranoid type, as well as their high-B blood group, which they brought with them from India (1948:175).

More recently, Hulse reaffirmed Kroeber's conclusion by observing,

> National, linguistic, religious, and class differences have also led to genetic distinctions between or within populations because of their influence upon the selection of mates. For example, in southern Spain, members of the upper classes are more likely to be blond than their lower class compatriots. . . . Gypsies have higher frequencies of B, R^1, and M blood types than their neighbors, as well as darker pigmentation (1963:367).

In spite of having long since been classified by physical anthropologists as Mediterranean Caucasoids (a racial classification they share in common with numerous non-Gypsy peoples), Andalusian Gypsies continue to adhere tenaciously to their traditional belief in their own racial distinctiveness. Indeed, it constitutes the main basis for their pronounced ethnocentrism and is supported in part by Garn's definition of "local races" as relatively small breeding populations whose limits are indicated "by cultural prohibitions on marriage outside of the group" (1961:17).

With respect to intelligence, the Gypsy's concern with outwitting the *busno* (non-Gypsy) has been credited with having motivated him to refine his powers of persuasion and to develop his keen powers of perception. Often described as a man of "instinct," lacking formal education, the Gypsy of Andalusia has been recognized throughout the centuries as being extremely astute, particularly in matters pertaining to his own survival and well-being. His exaggerated pride has communicated itself even to Andalusian non-Gypsies, who, in turn, are almost as ethnocentric about "their Gypsies" as the Gypsy, himself. On all sides the visitor is challenged to compare the physical beauty of the Andalusian Gypsies to any other group of Gypsies in the world. Not only do the Andalusians consider their Gypsies to be superior in physical type, but they believe them to be superior in innate intelligence, wit, and artistic ability as well. This form of ethnocentrism is reflected in the widespread use of the term "*¡Qué gitano!*" ("How Gypsy!") to express extreme approval or admiration of non-Gypsy people, acts, or things.

When it has been said that the Gypsy is not a "thinker," what has been meant generally is that the Gypsy seldom has tended to indulge in reflective or abstract thinking for the sake of thinking alone. First, history has shown that his mode of life has rarely freed him for this type of mental exercise. Second, Gypsy values have always centered primarily on discovering *practical* ways to make the most of, and to enjoy, the *present*, with scant value being placed upon abstract philosophical considerations. Whether by the *Hokkano Baró*, the successful evasion of early Spanish law, occultism, skillful horse trading, or whatever, down through history the Gypsy has exhibited a consistent and remarkable talent for outwitting, often at his own game, the *busno* in Spain. The success of the picaresque life of the Gypsy in Spain, now on the wane, has been shown by Starkie to have been the result of the Gypsy's intellectual agility, as well as what is most often described as his highly developed and "intuitive" understanding of human strengths and weaknesses. With respect to the latter, Starkie pointed out that the *caló* word *chanelar*, used by the Gypsies in Spain, has a far subtler meaning than its Spanish counterpart, *saber*; the former means "to know by intuition," while the latter means merely "to know" (1953:54–65). This, in essence, has been the line of distinction drawn by the Gypsy between his own intellectual abilities and those of the non-Gypsy, the principal basis for his long-held belief in the superiority of Gypsy mentality.

"THE EYES SING TO ME OF THE PERSON"

In spite of some exposure in this century to education and, more recently, to the mass media (television, radio, and so forth), our informants continue to emphasize innate rather than learned abilities. With few exceptions, superior Gypsy "talents" are explained as the result of heredity, usually expressed as a matter of either "blood" or "race"—"It is born in us." Asked about Gypsy fortune-telling, Isabel Fajardo-Maya, one of our principal Sacro Monte informants, explained,

> There are some who read it *in truth*. Those who can, they say, wept in their mother's womb and know everything. Those are the true ones. They take the talent from their mothers, like everything in life. They look at a person's face and know if he is good or bad. They read it there—Understand? When I tell the future, I only take account of the eyes—the eyes—they sing to me of the person—all I need to know.

"COUSIN—YOU ARE AS GYPSY AS THE RIBS OF GOD!"[1]

The cultural ethnocentrism of the Gypsies was found reflected by students of Gypsy culture not only in Gypsy law, to which reference will be made in the next section of this chapter, but in Gypsy origin tales as well. The following, first reported by Starkie, is a typical example of how this particaular form of oral tradition was used to reinforce the self-esteem and pride in group membership perpetuated by the Gypsies of Andalusia. As related by the Gypsy, Serafina, of Gaudix,

---

[1] Brown 1922:38.

The "Cales" believe that at the beginning of the world God made the "Busno" out of slime: then he made a woman out of the "Busno's" spare rib. Later on he found that the world was so dull with these two "Busnos" and their children that he said to himself—"I must liven things up." So one night, when the man was sleeping in his cave, God goes and takes a bit of his jaw-bone and in a twinkling of an eye he makes out of it a stiff and sturdy "Calorro" [Gypsy] alive and kicking (1937:364–365).

The famous prejudices of Gypsies against non-Gypsies has been seen by some to have been as much the outgrowth of the Gypsies' own fixed and traditional belief in their innate superiority as it is the result of negative experiences they encountered in their centuries of wandering from land to land. One such theory has held that, while the persecution and the betrayal of Gypsies by non-Gypsies operated to intensify the Gypsies' prejudices, such activities served more to prove to them the given fact of the physical, cultural, and moral inferiority of non-Gypsies than to create it. As a consequence, the receptiveness or lack thereof of Gypsies to strangers has been found to be directly related to the strangers' ability to show proof of Gypsy kinship ties, even if remote. This failing, on rare occasions Gypsies have utilized "blood-brother" and other ceremonies to establish fictive kinship ties with non-Gypsies. Starkie, many times over a "blood-brother" of the Gypsies, described one such ritual as follows:

Over our wine Lili, with his knife, pricked Pavo's finger and I sucked the blood from it after swallowing some bread dipped in salt. Then Lili pricked my finger and Pavo put it in his mouth to suck the blood after repeating the ceremony of the bread and salt. He then presented me with a rough silver ring and I gave him a pair of silver links I happened to have in my rucksack (1937:129).

Borrow, in a different vein, reported that some of the Gypsies among whom he worked accepted him on the basis of their belief that the soul which inhabited his body must have tenanted that of a Gypsy at some former period (1908:1). Brown, through his ability to speak caló, played the Gypsy role so convincingly that he was accepted on one occasion by the Gypsies of Granada as "a gitano de verdad, 'with seven ribs and a half,' like every real son of Egypt" (1922:7). Aside from these rather isolated instances, however, the Gypsy has maintained an aloofness from non-Gypsies regarding intratribal and familial relationships and affairs to which even his most violent critics have had to pay grudging respect.

With regard to the question of their superiority, Gypsies rarely are embarrassed by it; indeed, most evince surprise that such a self-evident fact requires corroboration. Recent Gypsy responses included: "Why do you ask this when you only have to open your eyes to see that it is so?" "All Gypsies know this, and are envied by the world for this reason." "To be born a Gypsy is the most that any man can wish. What man does not know this?" "Surely you who are intelligent know this to be true without asking."

Others noted: "It is given to Gypsies to see things that others do not see, even with all of their books and inventions." "Gypsies are seldom sick. We are born strong in all ways." "We Gypsies are loyal to our own, and protect our families." "Gypsies are more courageous than others, and bear pain in silence." "No Gypsy turns from another Gypsy in trouble." "Gypsy women are the most beautiful women in the world." (The last statement, from a seventy-four-year-old former dancer, was followed with the request that we send her cosmetics from the United States because "it is important that one keeps one's face pretty as one grows older.")

One informant concluded his statements by saying, "We live as men should live, close to nature and obedient to our laws."

Preeminence of Gypsy Law

The false Juanito, day and night
Had best with caution go
The Gypsy *carles* of Yeira height
Have sworn to lay him low.
Borrow 1908:293

As reported in recent times by one Spanish authority (Luna 1952:98), *"Los mandamientos de la ley calé son sencillos y rotundos:"*

1. *No te separas de los* rom.
2. *Guarda fidelidad a los* rom.
3. *Paga lo que debas a los* rom.

In essence this statement of Gypsy law is virtually identical with Borrow's notations made more than a century earlier (1908:27), "Gypsy law divides itself into the three following heads or precepts":

1. Separate not from *the husbands.*
2. Be faithful to *the husbands.*
3. Pay your debts to *the husbands.*

Close examination of these dictates revealed that they stressed, in the main, the maintenance of Gypsy separateness from non-Gypsy populations. The first, for example, enjoined the Gypsy not to live with non-Gypsies, as well as to conform to all aspects of the Gypsy way of life. The second, directed primarily at Gypsy women, discouraged marriage with non-Gypsies, and underlined the marital responsibilites of Gypsy women, complete faithfulness to their husbands being the foremost among them.

This was a very important injunction, so much so, indeed,

that upon the observance of it depended the very existence of the Romany sect— for if the female Gypsy admitted the *gorgio* [non-Gypsy] to the privilege of the Rom, the "race" of the Romany would quickly disappear (Borrow 1908:28).

While more particularly intended for women, this law also bade the male Gypsy to be faithful to his own people, and served to assure that Gypsy welfare would be placed above all other in contacts with non-Gypsies.

The third law established principles of honor to be observed within Gypsy tribal society, especially pertinent to the paying of debts owed by one Gypsy to another. It protected, too, Gypsy property rights, and insured that each Gypsy family accepted the responsibility of providing for its own needs.

The elders, Sacro Monte

As described by Block (1939:171–177) and others, traditionally, Gypsy law was administered by secret Gypsy tribunals (the *Kris*) consisting of tribal elders and Gypsy chiefs. Gypsies who had broken their laws, (for example, by stealing from another Gypsy, by violating a Gypsy woman, or by revealing tribal secrets) were summoned to appear before the tribunals for judgment of their crimes. Fines and punishments were imposed by the tribunals according to the gravity of each individual offense, the more serious crimes being punished by banishment from the tribe for periods ranging from a short time to life. No Gypsy could drink or travel with Gypsies thus declared "unclean" lest he fall under the same ban, and little or no pity was ever shown to condemned Gypsies, tribal justice being held always above question.

Laws relating to conjugal fidelity appear to have received more attention by gypsiologists than any others. They frequently call attention to Cervantes' description of them in his novel *La Gitanilla*, written in 1612. Presiding at the betrothal of a non-Gypsy to a Gypsy girl, the old Gypsy chief lays down the Romany doctrine in these words:

> Marry her, or choose any other you may desire, but once chosen you must not leave her for another. We keep inviolable the law of friendship, for no one covets what belongs to another, and we are devoid of the passion of jealousy. Cases of incest there are amongst us but none of adultery; and when it is our wife who is guilty, we do not go to justice for retribution; we ourselves are both judges and executioners of our wives if they are unfaithful (Starkie 1953:58).

Punishment for infidelity has been described as having assumed a variety of severe forms: public whippings, facial disfigurements, mutilations, and death all having been reported.

"THE GYPSY WOMAN NEVER CHEATS"

In recent work with Gypsy women, we have found that rather than resenting these ancient laws, they continue to support them and encourage their perpetuation in actual behavior as well as expressed ideal. A matter, also, of intense pride, the fidelity of Gypsy wives is used often as proof of the superiority of Gypsy culture. The following is a verbatim excerpt from a taped interview (Granada 1968) in which the subject is discussed with us by a Sacro Monte Gypsy mother and her daughter, both of whom, ironically, are married to non-Gypsies:

Carmen: The Gypsy woman for her husband has loyalty to the maximum.
Question: And the husbands?
Carmen: Also.
Probe: Many people do not believe that this is so.
            [Note: Mother joins conversation.]
Isabel: The love of a Gypsy is very different from the love of a Castilian—because there are Castilians who, at times, are living with their husbands but making love with other men. But among Gypsies that does not exist. The Gypsy woman takes her husband when she is a virgin—a person she really likes—for her *entire* life. If the husband is a drunk, doesn't make money—because he doesn't want to work—the Gypsy woman consents to look for work in order to "carry her home forward." Actually, the *gitana* doesn't want her husband to work too much. She wants him to work some, but she prefers to do the most work. She helps him a great deal—and if her husband were to be sick, she dies of pain. What she wants for her husband is a peaceful life—and she doesn't care if someone else can offer her many millions—even the most handsome man in the world.
Carmen: The Gypsy woman never cheats her husband.
Isabel: If he [the other man] says, "I like you a lot," she says, "This cannot be." For the Gypsy woman—*only* her husband. And there are Gypsies who, when their husbands die, for the rest of their lives remain without men. They live with their children, they live their Gypsy life. Some dance, others sell castanets—selling flowers—selling small copperware. That way they eat—and don't think bad things.

Other laws of the Gypsies which have been singled out for separate consideration by such writers as Borrow (1908:60) include those which forbid any Gypsy to eat, drink, or sleep in the house of a non-Gypsy, or to teach the Gypsy language to any but those who by birth or inauguration belonged to a Gypsy tribe. As noted previously, while neither widespread nor favored, on occasion non-Gypsies were, and continue to be, admitted to tribal membership; however, it has always remained obscure as to how all-encompassing the rights and privileges accorded these individuals ever become.

For example, if a non-Gypsy marries a Gypsy, he usually becomes subject to Gypsy law, with his offspring raised as Gypsies. The remark of a Gypsy woman married to a Spaniard that certain Gypsy traditions would have to be omitted from her daughter's wedding because she was not of "pure Gypsy blood" raises doubt that the offspring of such unions, even when sanctioned, are accorded full rights and privileges. When pressed for details, the girl's mother sadly stated that, even though she herself was a "pure" Gypsy, as was the girl's fiancé, the fact that

Copper vendor

the girl's father was not precluded the possibility of having a traditional Gypsy wedding following the church ceremony. However, she brightened considerably as she pointed out that her daughter's children would be far enough removed from their grandfather's "taint" to be eligible for the traditional ceremonies when they married as "they will be *pure* Gypsies in the eyes of other Gypsies." Further amplification of her own daughter's status, as well as that of her husband, was not forthcoming, and further questioning brought forth only the response, "It is the Gypsy way, and though it causes me much pain, it is the only right way."

The unquestioning loyalty and obedience of most Gypsies to their laws has been credited with having enabled them to maintain their ethnic distinctiveness, even though in some areas the administration of justice has been partially relinquished to local, non-Gypsy authorities.

As the Gypsies have become more sedentary, their total dependence on Gypsy law has given way, particularly in terms of punishment for crimes covered also by Spanish law, to increased dependence on local justice. Nevertheless, Gypsy law has continued to be accorded greater importance by the Gypsies than local law in matters pertaining to loyalty, ethnic "purity," and internal tribal affairs. For example, in instances where punishment by local authorities is considered inadequate, Gypsy law may impose additional penalties. This form of repunishment applies only to transgressions threatening Gypsy welfare and does not encompass other crimes, no matter how seriously regarded by non-Gypsies.

Throughout the years Gypsy informants have been more cautious in discussing their belief in the preeminence of Gypsy law than any other culture theme. In validation interviews fully one-third of the original Gypsy sample withheld opinions on it completely. Typical responses, some phrased in hostile or suspicious terms, included: "I do not think of these things. Are you being paid to find out?" "It is better not to answer. Who knows what might come of it." Other answers simply were stated as "I do not know," following which unrelated subjects usually were introduced as a way of changing the trend of the discussion.

The majority of Gypsy informants, however, were in agreement with the proposition, and, in sharp contrast to the evasiveness of those who withheld opinions, most of these appeared to be eager to discuss their opinions at length and in detail. One of the male elders of a Sacro Monte family stated, "Naturally we are first faithful to the laws of our own people, but we know too that it is best today to obey the local laws as well. Always we remember that Gypsy law is the best for us, in spite of changes we have seen. No *real* Gypsy places any other law higher." Another informant noted, "Gypsy law is ancient. To obey it is 'born' in us, so of course it is the most important law of all. Everything else does not matter when compared to protecting our ways and our 'race.' This is what our law does." A third informant, also of the Sacro Monte, pointed out, "Gypsy law is the same for all, whether rich or poor. To help one's brother, to be faithful to our own, and to obey *el mayor, el que manda* [the eldest male of the family, he who orders]—what better way is there?"

It was noted that the following three principal ideas tended to be stressed by all Gypsy informants who believed in the preeminence of their laws: (1) Gypsy law acts as a cohesive force serving to protect Gypsy interests, rights, traditions, and ethnic distinctiveness; (2) Gypsy law is more democratic than any other law because it does not discriminate against individuals without financial or other influence; and (3) because Gypsy law has maintained its basic form, even though older methods of punishment have given way largely to banishment or social

Joaquín:
"El que manda"

ostracism, it must be more nearly perfect than other laws, which appear to be undergoing constant change. Relative to the last item, a Gypsy from Cordoba stated, "Our laws are known to us all. Who can keep up with changes in laws made by the government or the Church?"

Albeit a minority, some male informants of the Sacro Monte, stressing the need to keep abreast of "modern times," questioned the highly resistant quality of Gypsy law. One said, "Local laws now protect us. There is no longer need for the laws which were necessary in the days when we were chased and denied safety." Actually, however, even these informants stressed their own faithfulness to those aspects of the old laws which protect internal Gypsy relationships. Their negations, or expressed desire for change, were found to focus primarily on laws regulating or restricting external affairs, especially those influencing Gypsy/non-Gypsy business interests.

Gypsy Loyalty

> Don't speak harshly of Gypsies,
>   For if you do,
> You bring dishonor on your own
>   Royal Gypsy blood.
>   Quintana 1960:196

Traditionally, the theme of loyalty in Gypsy culture has tended to overlap with other cultural themes. As already indicated, it has been reflected in both Gypsy law and ethnocentrism. Even those whose writings evinced hostile attitudes toward Gypsies singled out this particular theme for special consideration. For example, the unknown author of a handwritten eighteenth-century manuscript owned by Starkie cautioned all non-Gypsies to learn the Gypsy language as a protective device. Believing Gypsies to constitute a "noxious and undesirable race," he felt that this was one way by which Spaniards might survive chance encounters with them. Inherent in this exposé of Gypsy customs and language, however, was the begrudging recognition of the strong bonds of loyalty which operated to keep outsiders from penetrating Gypsy strongholds, or learning their secrets.

Ironically, Borrow, who forecast the ethnic extinction of Gypsies, presented some of the most mitigatory arguments against their total assimilation. He was among the first (1842) to draw attention to the theme of loyalty in Gypsy culture. In a later study, he again drew attention to this theme as expressed by the chastity of Gypsy women, the famous *lacha y trupos* (virginity) of the *gitanas* (1908:266–273).

Brown, in writing of a Gypsy wedding in Malaga, again focused interest on the Gypsy emphasis on loyalty and chastity by referring to the traditional ceremony of the *diklo*. He wrote,

> It [the ceremony of the *diklo*] consists in ascertaining by means of a handkerchief whether or not the bride is still a virgin. This is usually performed by the groom's mother. In former times she exhibited to the [wedding] guests the *diklo* with its crimson stains (1929:97).

Still later, Starkie contributed to the literature the following detailed description of a wedding which took place among the cave-dwelling Gypsies of Benalúa:

> The supreme spree of the Benalúa Gypsies is the marriage *fiesta* which must be carried out according to the Romany ritual. . . . They marry in the tribe before the old men. The ceremony resembles that of Guadix and Granada. The *novio*, once he has made up his mind to marry the girl, carries her off from her parents. The parents pretend to be very angry and a mock fight is often staged. They do not, however, allow the *novio* to consummate the marriage until the following night. When the marriage has been consummated an old woman called the *picaora* goes in and takes the nightdress of the *novia* and shows it bloodstained to the crowd of relatives and guests. . . . The tribe must be sure that the bride is a virgin, hence the importance of the *picaora*, who is charged with the task of seeing that the girl is truly *intacta*. The *fiesta* cannot begin until the *picaora* has announced her verdict. In some parts of Spain the *picaora* lets off as a signal a dove just before she hoists the white *diklo* (1937:381–382).

Penalties for infidelity are unusually severe among Gypsies; for example, the woman may lose even her right to a name.

> You are not called Carmen
> Nor Maria, nor Pilar;
> Each day you may be called
> Whatever they wish
> For being a woman of the street.
> Cimorra 1943:114

Among sedentary Andalusian Gypsies, the ceremony of the *diklo* is rarely performed today. Nevertheless, even our most recent field data support the fact that the rigid norms it exemplified continue to govern premarital and marital sexual behavior. One informant stated to us that her people wanted no "gifts" of sexual promiscuity from non-Gypsies; another pointed out that the virginity of Gypsy brides still was the basis for Gypsy familial and ethnic loyalty.

> Family loyalty is a prominent characteristic of Gypsies. Combined with their love of procreation, this devotion to a small group is probably the reason why they have survived so long, with all their peculiar characteristics, among nations which were strange to them (Block 1939:175).

"NO FAIR TEARING CLOTHES OR MENTIONING MOTHERS"

Family loyalty among Gypsies is particularly manifested in the mother–son relationship. Starkie notes a folktale concerning the fate of a Gypsy wife who had incurred the displeasure of her mother-in-law. As the young wife met death at the hands of her husband, he cried out, "Many a wife can I find in the world, but I have only one mother" (1937:116–117). Brown observed that, among small Gypsy boys of Cadiz, there existed a formula before starting a tussle which cautioned, "No fair tearing clothes or mentioning mothers" (1929:70). Similarly, he reported that, among adult Gypsy males, an insult known to have resulted in death for persons uttering it was the phrase, "¡*Puta tu mare*! [Your mother's a whore!]."

The importance of the mother–son motif in Gypsy culture is perhaps best illustrated in the content of Gypsy Deep Song. Expressed in terms of the loyalty of sons to their mothers rather than the reverse pattern, numerous *coplas* (folk poems or songs) have been recorded emphasizing this theme. One of the *coplas* sung by the late Manuel Centeno, a leading exponent of Deep Song, expressed this theme in terms of the greater sorrow felt by Gypsies at the death of a mother than that of a father.

> When a mother dies,
>   Four columns of marble break.
> When a father dies,
>   Only one.
>   Quintana 1960:189

Cimorra, in his definitive work, devotes an entire section to the mother motif in Deep Song, calling it one of the most often repeated of the various themes encountered. He called the cry "¡*Ay mi madre!*" the universal cry of wounded humanity, and noted that this "truth" was echoed in the songs (1943:95).

Regarding the loyalty of Gypsies to Gypsies, virtually all authorities since Borrow frequently have alluded to this theme. "No matter how kind you are to them," said one Spanish informant recently, "Gypsies first, last, and always, are interested only in the welfare of other Gypsies. So, be on guard lest they fool you into thinking otherwise." Another, a former dancer who had employed numerous Gypsy performers in her professional work, noted that her experiences with them had repeatedly illustrated their loyalty to their immediate families and kin. Citing numerous cases, she pointed out that money she gave Gypsy performers for medical treatment, for clothes, or for other necessities more often than not was turned over to family elders for equal distribution. So widespread was this practice that she finally found it necessary to appoint a non-Gypsy to supervise expenditures in order to insure that the Gypsy performers were adequately protected. In addition, she reported that Gypsy performers not infrequently feigned illness and other misfortunes in order to extract more money from her to channel back to their families, from whom they were separated by both time and distance.

This is not to say, however, that Gypsy loyalties are never extended beyond their own ethnic group. In the somewhat rare instances in which non-Gypsies are accepted into their homes, they have been found to identify closely with their safety and interests. The lay belief that Gypsies are fickle and totally incapable of establishing lasting rapport with outsiders is both inaccurate and misleading. Violations of friendships are denounced vehemently by them. A *gitana* in Madrid, alluding to a Gypsy woman who had cruelly exploited a non-Gypsy friend, said, "She is bad for all Gypsies. It is our law that friends be treated well. All of us suffer when one such as she betrays a good friend." Although the story, still widely circulated, contained elements of sexual deviancy, it appeared that the betrayal of friendship was considered to be the more serious of the two issues.

In our experiences with the Fajardo-Maya Gypsies of Granada's Sacro Monte, a fictive kin relationship has evolved over a decade which is characterized by trust, affection, and deep involvement, not only with ourselves, but also with members of our families, only one of whom they have ever met. The crimes of which Gypsies are accused, the *Hokkano Baró* and similar acts attributed to them, are, to the best of our intimate knowledge, principally kept alive by tourist guides anxious to thrill their clients.

Five out of every six Gypsy informants agreed that the theme of loyalty constituted one of the principal themes around which their culture was oriented. In general, reasons advanced concerning the importance of this particular theme in the culture were vague and tended to be emotionally overtoned. Typical responses included such statements as: "We know that the Gypsy way is best. We teach our children to be loyal to their own kind. We turn our backs on those who break this law." "The purity of our daughters and the faithfulness of our wives has long surprised strangers; all ask about these things, but we would die to keep it so." "You have only to sit with us, to see that no other people are so united and devoted to one another in these times. Yet, it has always been so." "Naturally, sisters and brothers fight, but they are loyal, and no brother would permit anyone to molest his sister. It is his duty, as that of his grandfathers before him, to protect the home and his own." "A Gypsy's wedding is the most important thing in life. It prepares the way for continuing family loyalty which is the basis for everything else." "Everyone envies us our ability to love and to remain loyal to one another. We are *born* that way, even though some Gypsies turn to other ways. We do not consider them as worthy of notice."

A male informant in Granada attributed to loyalty the vital consequence of internal strength and unity.

> Our loyalty to one another has permitted us to survive throughout all periods of our existence. It will continue to be so. Even though we are sometimes small in number, none are stronger than we in these matters. While we are in some way unlike those [Gypsies] before us, some among us even being unwilling to help his *cousins* in trouble, for the most part, we have changed little. The young continue the ways taught them by the elders because they know that respect and love of family, and loyalty to those of their own kind, will continue and strengthen the *race* [italics ours].

No Gypsy informant disagreed that loyalty continued to constitute a theme in their culture, although some questioned its endurance in the face of change. One stated, "Things are changing. There are things which cause us to wonder whether loyalty is as important today as *duros* [dollars] in the pocket." Another, reflecting upon the increase in the numbers of Gypsies engaged in outside occupations, asked, "Will not this weaken our bonds to one another, causing us to abandon old loyalties and to form new ones?"

Similar concerns were expressed by the majority of non-Gypsy informants, one of whom charged that the Gypsies had been "spoiled" by the acclaim accorded their dancing, singing, and other folk arts. "As the Gypsy has become more dependent upon non-Gypsies for his bread and butter," went the characteristic argument in this category, "he cares less for other Gypsies than in the past. The old loyalties are disappearing except those related to marriage. In this, the Gypsy remains, as always, devoted to his wife and children."

These concerns notwithstanding, Gypsies continue to view the theme of loyalty as remaining relatively constant in their culture. Described as a man of deep feelings and affections, the Gypsy, often at his own expense, has maintained his loyalty to his own kin and to his own ethnic group. The resultant cohesiveness characteristic of Gypsy culture has proceeded as much from the internalized value placed on the transmission and perpetuation of the loyalty theme which reinforced it as from any identifiable need occasioned by outside pressure. This is not to say, however, that the original value placed by the Gypsies upon loyalty to their own members developed in a cultural vacuum; rather it is to denote that whatever the original external forces behind its development, it assumed intrinsic, as well as functional, worth.

Gypsy Freedom

Cut from Heaven's tree
I have twin leaves, see!
One says, "You are poor."
One says, "You are free!"
Brown 1929:160

The value placed by the Gypsies on their freedom has been the most publicized and romanticized of all themes in Gypsy culture. Frequently the subject of poets, essayists, and others, Baudelaire, Browning, Cervantes, Keats, Eliot, and Pushkin, to identify but a few, the roaming life and freedom of the Gypsy has found expression in a variety of literary forms. While these often reflect more the personal longings of their authors than those of their Gypsy subjects, the more precise and objective works of gypsiologists also have emphasized the freedom theme. It has been reported from a number of viewpoints, among them those which have encompassed such topics as Gypsy antimilitarism, the effects of confinement upon the Gypsy, the Gypsy emphasis on pleasure and idleness, and the reluctance of Gypsies to be bound by conventionalized forms of behavior found in non-Gypsy populations.

Brown, in his most famous Gypsy study, observed that "for a Gypsy, compulsory military service is almost as bad as jail" (1929:43). More recently, in personal correspondence, Starkie referred to the Gypsy practice of declaring male children as females in order to avoid military service (1959). These pronounced antimilitaristic attitudes have been observed to stem neither from fear nor from ideological rejection of physical force but rather from the restrictive conditions of such service. The Gypsy, while never accorded particular recognition for services rendered during periods of conflict in Spanish history (it being doubtful that they were ever of major significance), nevertheless has been noted for both his courage and his ability to cope with situations requiring independent action. It appears that freedom from formalized restrictions has been the main prerequisite for efficient functioning on the part of the Gypsy in times of stress, although there is little documented evidence to support this generally accepted belief. The fact is that Gypsies in uniform are rarities in Spain, and the number of Gypsies conscripted for military service always has been small and of minor import.

In a similar vein, the Gypsy's aversion to confinement of any type has caused a number of Gypsy scholars to examine attitudes toward imprisonment.

A modern Gypsy picaroon

The most serious negative effects of imprisonment seem to result from solitary confinement rather than from harsh physical treatment or deprivation. Brown noted that confinement was harder for a Gypsy to bear than for any other man. "For this reason," he added, "there was an old law in Rumania which gave the Gypsies a lighter sentence than others" (1929:40). Borrow, too, alluded frequently to the effects of imprisonment on Gypsies, stressing particularly in his work the duty of other Gypsies to assist Gypsy prisoners (1908:216–219).

The theme of freedom also is reflected in traditional occupations, many of which were developed with the express purpose of providing Gypsies with means of livelihood which would neither commit them to any one place nor to any one type of employment. Fortune-telling, horse trading, itinerant metalworking, begging, basketry, all of the various tricks associated with the "picaresque life," and even Gypsy folk arts, served to meet the Gypsy demand for income without loss of freedom. These skills also served to insure their survival in the days when, as hunted outcasts, they were denied safety in sedentary occupations. In addition, the Gypsy emphasis on pleasure rather than on money—"*'Er gusto bale má que er dinero'*" [Pleasure, whim is worth more than money] (Brown 1929:44)— led to the need for free periods of idleness to allow time both for pleasurable indulgences and for the accumulation of the reserves of energy needed to sustain them. In Brown's words:

But Gypsies are never satisfied with extremes, they must transcend them, they must whip their passions with all their might, and beat against the final barrier. Periods of depression follow, and long intervals of utter idleness and relaxation, oblivious to all inner and outer compulsion, dreaming, laughing, and accumulating the great reserves of energy that they swiftly empty in a few hours or a few nights and days of fun (1929:86).

Referring to the modern Gypsy picaroon, Starkie has pointed out that "the humblest Gypsy picaroon in Seville and the most blue-blooded noble still have this in common: both firmly believe that to work for the sake of work is to be unworthy of the dignity of man" (1953:65). An aged dancer, in an especially candid response to our questions about the freedom theme in Gypsy culture, said, "To be free, to have money, to live well, and not to work are the things we prize most." So self-evident did she believe this to be that she called the question "tontería" (foolish, stupid), an adjective which seemed also, in her opinion, to include any anthropologist who felt it necessary to ask it in the first place!

Conversely, some female respondents indicated that, as Gypsies have moved into occupations either formerly denied them, or now more highly organized, freedom no longer constituted as vital an issue in their lives as previously. One stated, "This freedom is a matter for Gypsies of the road. We are no longer interested in such a life with all of its hardships. The kind of freedom we value is that which comes with food on the table and money coming in." Another said, "We look now to steady jobs rather than to singing of freedom." It was noted that the attitudes of these informants corresponded rather closely with the observation made earlier relative to the economic importance of women in the support of the home. As one informant stated, "Men have more time to indulge in fantasies about freedom. Women have to worry about the table."

In contrast to the responses just reported, no male Gypsy informant believed that modern practical considerations precluded the possibility of their continuing to transmit and perpetuate the freedom theme; indeed, some even believed that these considerations facilitated the process. One said, "Our freedom is more important today than ever. I would say that we are freer than those who travel all of the time. In some ways we have changed outwardly, but we remain inwardly the same." Another reported, "The things you [referring to non-Gypsies] see are not the important ones. While we may seem to have given up freedom in return for other things, this is not so. Even our children know that to be free, as we have been always, es la finalidad de la vida [is the ultimate aim of life]." Some informants independently cited the Gypsy toast "¡salú y libertá!" in support of their affirmative responses, while others held that the Gypsy emphasis on freedom was the most important factor distinguishing the Gypsy from the non-Gypsy in Spain. In summary, Gypsies who supported the proposition appeared to regard freedom as a cultural goal which, regardless of the necessity to conform superficially to some of the freedom-limiting demands of modern life, continued to be intrinsically valuable and worthy of being maintained in their culture.

The majority of non-Gypsy informants considered the theme of freedom still to be the most important in Gypsy culture. They stressed the timelessness of the theme itself, the general tendency of the Gypsies to avoid occupations which require the sacrifice of freedom, the "quicksilverish" Gypsy approach toward responsibility, and the reluctance of Gypsies to identify their interests with those of non-Gypsies, even for practical considerations. Said one informant, "Once the Gypsy has made enough money to go on a spree, or to provide for his immediate needs, off he goes. His freedom today is still his most important prized possession, and he very seldom considers tomorrow." This observation was supported in our 1968 studies of Gypsy aspirations, especially with regard to attitudes toward work, money, *alegría*, and time. Albeit modified, the essence of the Gypsy life style continues to be summed up in the love of freedom.

Gypsy Fatalism

I hope God never gives,
Even to those I hate,
Such sorrows as he sent to me
Such evil, evil fate.
Brown 1929:155

As viewed by recognized authorities, the theme of Gypsy fatalism has assumed two related forms: the emphasis placed by the Gypsies on relating the joys and sorrows of the past to those of the present and the preoccupation of the Gypsy with the death theme. As noted in Chapter 2, one of the strongest arguments the *gitano* and the *andaluz* had for accepting each other was their mutual recognition and understanding of the paradox of joy and sadness. Starkie (1953:97) was among those who noted that the melancholy of the *andaluz* was underlined by that of the Gypsy, who, the *andaluz* said, *"tiene la alegría de estar triste"* (rejoices in being sad).

The belief of the Gypsies that the happenings of the past are inseparable from those of the present has been credited with having accentuated their resistance to change, on the one hand, and with having had a strengthening effect on their powers of endurance, on the other. In comparing Gypsy fatalism to that of "most Orientals," Brown observed that

> they [the Gypsies] submit to the harshest circumstances without a murmur. Nature and destiny have made them philosophical. "Only dogs and *Gajos* get mad," I once heard a Gypsy say.
> This does not mean, however, that they are stolid. Extreme mobility of temperament is a prominent trait. Though they bow to the inevitable, they are very passionate, and have quick tempers (1922:20–21).

Block, similarly, noted that the basis of a Gypsy's life is his "unquestioning trust in the working of the Universe, the rightness of which it would never occur to a Gypsy to doubt. For this reason he is never discontented with life. He takes it for granted, and accepts the fact that it cannot be different from what it is" (1939:195). This particular quotation is significant in pointing out that Gypsy fatalism and sadness are not completely synonymous terms, although they are intimately associated with one another. As interpreted by a number of scholars, Gypsy fatalism has served to remove certain elements of doubt and stress from the Gypsy's round of life, thereby freeing him to pursue pleasures of the moment rather than activities calculated to insure a better future.

Brown's observations (1929:43–49) that "Gypsies are not content with spending their last cent: in order to be happy they must defy all sense of practicality" and the Gypsy saying "We live on song and die of it" are also reflections of the fatalistic attitude of the Gypsy toward his destiny. If events *do* happen repeatedly, "as in the *coplas*," there is little need, the argument has run, for either abstract planning or for the conservation of personal and material strengths and energies against the needs of another day. However, because Gypsy life, contrary to the notion prevalent among romanticists, has been both difficult and tragic, it is not possible in treating this subject to ignore the fact that there has always been an undercurrent of melancholy and sadness in Gypsy fatalism. Because of its intangibility, this aspect of Gypsy fatalism has tended to be obscured by more purely pleasurable manifestations of fatalistic belief in the culture and, accordingly, has both escaped and defied adequate analysis.

The Gypsy preoccupation with the theme of death, closely related to fatalism, has been expressed in a number of Gypsy activities, not the least of which have been their performing folk arts. In referring to the fact that the Gypsy singer is "obsessed by the death theme," Starkie noted that the Gypsy brought the quality of sadness into *cante jondo*, or Deep Song, "which has been very well defined by García Sánchez as 'the drama of humanity in chains'" (1953:97). Brown also called attention to the fact that the Gypsies frequently transmuted grief into happiness by the alchemy of song, quoting, by way of illustration, the Gypsy *copla*, "My heart has more sorrows than anyone can know and for that reason it is a nest of songs" (1929:187–188).

Gypsy wakes and funerals have been described as "frenzied" affairs. Both Starkie and Block have contributed to the literature descriptive and interpretive data concerning the many and varied customs associated with them. Among these, the absence of prolonged periods of mourning was noted to correspond to the Gypsy acceptance of what life forces upon the individual, although it was stressed that a suitable funeral, accompanied by weeping and loud lamentations, was considered to be essential, both to afford enjoyment to the dead and to insure the departure of the soul (Block 1939:198). Starkie, in a somewhat different vein, reported that a Gypsy of Guadix explained the orgy of gaiety in honor of the dead (in this instance, a child) in the following terms:

> Why shouldn't they jump for joy and shout and dance? The child was lucky to die so early. Have we *Cales* so much to be thankful for in life? What a deal of sorrow and suffering that child has escaped (1937:362).

The Gypsy's skillful adaptation to the *corrida* (bullfight) also has been attributed to his fatalistic outlook. One writer concluded that "only a child of the soil may act in such a drama, a drama of Death and Fate, the image of life, over which broods relentlessly the end that none may escape" (Brown 1922:242).

Throughout the years, our work with Andalusian Gypsies has revealed that the paradoxes of sorrow and joy, self-pity and stoicism, conservatism and excessive indulgence, are all variously associated with the fatalistic orientation of their

Contrasting Gypsy Moods

"Alegría"

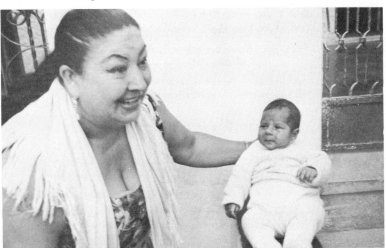

"Mal tiempo"

culture. Not surprisingly, responses to questions concerning fatalism reflected the same paradoxical qualities or contradictions just noted. Although only half of our Gypsy informants agreed that fatalistic attitudes continue to dominate in their culture, prolonged contact with them raised serious doubts as to the validity of negative responses.

Typical responses given by informants in agreement wtih the proposition included the following: "There is no use in running after luck [*la dicha*]. What will be, will be. That is the way of our life." "A man's destiny [*hado*] cannot be changed. It is foolishness to try." "I find very boresome [*muy aburrido*] the thing of always seeking, seeking. I live for today, the things of tomorrow don't bother me." "We live, we die; what does it matter. The end is always the same." As noted, the responses in this category contained frequent references to such concepts as "luck," "fate," and "predestination."

Informants disagreeing gave responses ranging from very simple to somewhat complex. Two merely stated that they did not believe that Gypsies were fatalistic. Another, after declaring that Gypsies were keeping up with changing times, noted that "only those who are lazy do not believe in a better life." Some informants believed that education made it possible for Gypsies today to improve their "luck" and condition. One said, "All this of fate and luck is of the past."

A Sacro Monte Gypsy singer cited her experience with modern medical treatment for a throat ailment as an example that "today we do not have to submit to fate. My throat was cured by penicillin; luck has nothing to do with it." More recently, however, the same informant in discussing related throat surgery performed by a Madrid specialist stated, "Imagine the feeling that it gave me that this doctor had accidentally passed through my cave. This must have been written by *fate*." Explaining that the doctor had told her to "forget the song," she added, "But we are *born* with this. You have only to look at me. It is my *curse* to sing. . . such *fate* [italics ours]."

"No opinion" responses concerning fatalism reflected, in the main, vacillation between the old and the new. A young Gypsy dancer, who had advanced the information that he was taking guitar lessons as insurance against the day when his "legs grew old," stated, "I was taught to believe that nothing could be changed, that all was ordered, but I do not know if this is so any longer." Confused by evidence which seemed contradictory to them, several respondents either withheld opinions or qualified them. A characteristic answer was, "Who can say for sure today. Some things are a man's destiny, they are foretold for him. I do not say 'yes' or 'no' to your question."

Among non-Gypsy informants, the Gypsy's lack of foresightedness, his traditional rejection of formal education, and his excesses in terms of spending and pleasure were cited most often as illustrative of his fatalistic "nature." However, we found social workers and teachers who contended that Gypsies today were in the process of adopting to modern technology and educational opportunities, which, in their opinion, either negated the Gypsy belief in fate or at least weakened it.

The ambivalent status of this theme in contemporary Andalusian Gypsy culture was perhaps best expressed by the Gypsy chief who asked, "Who can say if we believe in fate or not? We die of it, and we live in spite of it."

4

Gypsy Deep Song

See for yourselves the transcendental quality of *cante jondo.* . . . It is deep
. . . deeper than the present heart that composes it or sings it, because it is
almost infinite. It comes from distant races, crossing the cemetery of the years
and the leaves of the shriveling winds. Born of the first cry. . . .

Federico García Lorca

THE USE OF DEEP SONG *coplas* to introduce the traditional themes presented in the preceding chapter, and to illustrate their cultural tenacity, already may have suggested to the reader the relevance of this form of oral tradition to the transmission and perpetuation of the thematic content of Andalusian Gypsy culture. This chapter should be viewed as an extension to the chapter on themes, with the focus on song and dance as vital expressions of dynamic cultural properties. A traditional folk art, the complex known as Deep Song has been preserved, enhanced, and used by Gypsies more than by any other Andalusian group.

Utilizing the anthropological definitions of the terms "form," "meaning," "use," and "function," sections devoted to each of these concepts are subdivided according to the elements which most closely relate to them. Thus, in the discussion of forms, topics considered are those pertinent to the general musical characteristics of Deep Song, the artifacts used in connection with it, the nature of the songs (that is, traditional, modern, or improvised), and the manner in which, and by whom, they are learned. The motifs of Deep Song are examined in the consideration of meaning, while the occasions and conditions under which it is sung are described in the discussion of use. In connection with function, the purposes of Deep Song, as viewed within Andalusian Gypsy culture, and the value placed upon it by the Gypsies are examined. Kroeber distinguished between these concepts mainly by attributing to form, meaning, and use a more objective or apparent quality than he attributed to function. Of the last he wrote that "function is something that the student or analyst of culture finds out about. Function is an interpretation, . . ." (1948:306). It is essentially in this context that the terms are used in the sections that follow.

Theories of Origin

The term "Deep Song" (*cante jondo, cante gitano, cante grande*, all three terms being used synonymously in Spain) refers to the most authentic and traditional song form of the Gypsies of Andalusia. This is not to say that Deep Song originated in its entirety with the Gypsies, or that it is necessarily their exclusive property. As reported by Torner, *cante jondo* has been assigned Gypsy paternity due to the fact that it lives and is cultivated *primarily* among them (1944:38). Recognizing the pronounced tendency of the Gypsy to perpetuate and embellish rather than to create, virtually all authorities subscribe to the theory that the *jondo* style actually evolved from *several* main streams of influence, of which the Gypsy influence was but one.

In a pamphlet long considered to be out of print (but found to be appended to another work) Manuel de Falla examined the question of *jondo* paternity, providing scholars and students with what appears to be the most generally accepted theory of origin. The pamphlet, issued in connection with the now-historic Deep Song Festival of 1922, sponsored by Falla and a committee of artists in Granada, contains a survey of pertinent historic factors, and an analysis of the musical elements of *jondo*. Of the former, Falla wrote that primitive Andalusian music was influenced by three main factors: (1) the adoption of Byzantine liturgical chants by the Church in Spain, (2) the Arab invasion, and (3) the arrival and settlement of numerous Gypsy bands in Spain (1950:121–147). He maintained that Byzantine and Arab elements fused with primitive Andalusian music to form the original basis of *cante jondo*, but attributed to the Gypsy the introduction of still new and independent elements which utimately resulted in the *jondo* style as known today.

Starkie, in commenting and building upon this theory, noted that once the Gypsies had absorbed the Andalusian style, they began to transform it in accordance with their own temperament. Among the Gypsy elements noted in *cante jondo*, the repetition of the same note "to the point of obsession," for example, has been compared with certain forms of enchantment. In connection with this observation, Starkie pointed out that the Gypsies incorporated into their singing "an intensity of expression" and a "barbaric strength" which was not unlike those qualities they had developed in casting spells, working the Great Trick, or telling fortunes (1953:96).

Musicologists tend to be in general agreement that the Gypsy musical idiom was rooted in a tradition not unlike that of Andalusia, a fact which enabled the Gypsy to master quickly the Hispano-Arabic music he found there and also to contribute toward its development. As a result, the Gypsy not only transformed his own songs and dances but those of the Andalusian as well. In the process, Brown added, many of the songs were fused to the end that "one hears them sing various types of song, some Spanish, some Gypsy, some so blended that one cannot say whether they are one or the other" (1929:19). Relative to this point, it is interesting that the use of Gypsy words by non-Gypsies in their songs, and the even more frequent use of Spanish words by Gypsies, no doubt contributed even further to the difficulties encountered in determining origin. "Here," wrote Brown, "language is not a safe guide. Spanish is the usual speech of nearly all *gitanos*, and most Spaniards know at least some Gypsy, for a goodly portion of Spanish slang comes from the Romani" (1929:22).

Persistent references may also be found in studies of Deep Song to the probable influence of Jewish music in its evolution. One such theory, authored by Medina Azara and reported by Starkie, held that the *cante jondo* of Spain derived in part from the holy festival songs of the Jews (1937:83). In support of this theory, analogies have been drawn between the chants of the Jews and Deep Song which show existing similarities between them; for example, in the voice modulations employed, and in the sound of the repeated "ay" common to both. While the actual degree of Jewish influence on the music of Moslem Spain is difficult to establish, it seems highly unlikely that in at least a half-century of coexistence in Andalusia the Jew and Gypsy did not engage in some form of two-way musical exchange.

In summary, while recognizing and accepting the fact that musicologists have yet to unravel all of the mysteries shrouding its origins, the Deep Song of the Andalusian Gypsies clearly appears to have evolved in its present form from the *cante primitivo* of Andalusia, the latter of which had already undergone synthesis with Byzantine and Arabic elements. Out of this base, which nurtured the elements contributed to it by the Gypsies, grew the *jondo* style—neither "pure" Andalusian nor "pure" Gypsy but, rather, a blend in which, in the words of Federico García Lorca, "the emotion of history, its lasting light without dates or facts, takes refuge" (1957:13).

Form of Deep Song

GENERAL MUSICAL CHARACTERISTICS

Written descriptions of Deep Song, like underexposed photographs, are little more than suggestive of their subject. A subjective analysis, written by Pritchett, expressed one type of effect of Deep Song on the newly initiated when he described it as

> . . . a new cadence, haunting, monotonous, yet also of pronounced dramatic rhythm. It is the rhetoric of music, sometimes tragic and grave, sometimes swanking and feverish with a swirl of skirts in it, sometimes Oriental, lyrical and sad. The ear catches the strange notes of the cadence at once—la, sol, fa, mi—in the singing voice or in the guitar. . . .
>
> Frequently, the songs are sung privately, for the singers' own consolation. For, despite its howling, it is also an intimate music, perhaps for a singer and a couple of friends only. It can be sung in a mere whisper. . . . One seems to be listening to a sudden, lyrical or passionate statement or exclamation, torn out of the heart of the singer (1954:127–135).

Attempts at more objective and informed description have been complicated principally by the fact that Deep Song has evaded musical notation to the extent that

> . . . it is virtually impossible to convey a faithful impression of *cante jondo* melody through the medium of our modern European musical notation, because of the chromatic inflections and subdivisions, and because of the free rhythm which does not conform to a regular measurement. Hearing a good *cante jondo* singer, such as "La Niña de los Peines," is the only way of becoming acquainted with the real spirit of this "deep song" (Chase 1941:225).

As might be assumed, few examples of genuine Deep Song are found in the literature, a notable exception being the collection of songs in the work of Eduardo Torner (1944:II). Even these, however, are fragmentary approximations of their prototypes, and suffer in transcription due to the peculiarities of Deep Song. Among these, Brown noted the multiplicity of rhythms and cross-rhythms, the complexity and fluidity of melodic themes, the use of microtones, grace notes, and the "flowing glide," the indifference to the quality of tone, the lack of a harmonized accompaniment, and the high degree of embellishment (1929:118–125).

Differences in systems of classifying the various types of songs exist, although, in the main, they tend to be differences in terms of detailed versus broad, general categorization. The two principal breakdowns are *cante flamenco* or *chico* ("little" song), constituted of less profound and lighter textured songs than those categorized as *cante jondo* or *grande* ("great" song). Under the former are classified *alegrías*, *bulerías*, *fandangos gitanos*, *malagueñas*, and the like. While these songs are generally more joyous than those of *cante jondo*, many contain within them the same brooding quality of the purer and more ancient styles.

The deepest and oldest of the Great Songs are represented by the *siguiriyas gitanas* (weeping songs) and the *soleares* (songs of solitude). Gypsy singers, with few exceptions, have been the acknowledged masters of the *siguiriyas gitanas*, songs profoundly expressive of human anguish and sadness. Describing the singing of a *siguiriya gitana*, Starkie wrote,

> The first two lines of the song were the defiance: the long third line started at the same high-pitched note, but the singer then prolonged the notes in breathless, descending vocalization, and at the end it seemed as if they would never die, for the shouts of "olé" and claps of the audience revived the dying voice into yet another turn and trill. . . . They were all passionately sad songs . . . (1935:275).

The *soleares*, considered by some to be the primitive archetype of both *cante grande* and *chico*, are filled with declarations of torment and tragedy. Manuel Machado, the Andalusian poet, described the *soleares* as the *madre del canto popular* (the mother of folk song), the deepest of all songs.

Of special importance in Gypsy culture, the *martinete* and its refined relative, the *debla*, were more recent additions to the *jondo* family. These are the so-called Deep Songs of the forge, the rhythms of which some authorities maintain were derived from the hammerings of metalworking Gypsies on their anvils. The late Manuel Centeno, one of Spain's most eminent masters of Deep Song styles, advanced the theory that the rhythms of these songs were, in fact, derived from the workings of the bellows used to keep the fires burning under the anvils rather than from the hammering itself (Quintana 1960:177).

Rosa Durán: "El baile jondo"

Deep Song: *Siguiriya gitano*

Manuel Centeno: "The sound of weeping"

Another group of "true" *cantes* are the *saetas*, which are usually sung to the style of the *martinete* or *siguiriya*. These "arrows of song" punctuate the Holy Thursday and Good Friday processions which fill Andalusian streets during Holy Week. The lonely singer standing in the doorway is said to duplicate the agony of Christ's ordeal on Mount Calvary as he spontaneously addresses his own grief to the passing Saints carried in procession. A particularly beautiful *saeta* sung by Isabel Fajardo-Maya, and poorly recorded on a hand-held tape recorder during the 1970 Holy Week observance in Granada, lingers still in memory. Asked to retape it in June, Isabel replied, "This cannot be. It was of that moment only. My *saeta* was a Holy thing." Expressive of their deepest emotions, the *saetas* of Gypsy singers are among the most moving of all of their songs.

In spite of the fact that one hears more *cante flamenco* (the commercial *zambras* of Granada's Gypsies, for example, rarely including *cante grande*), all Gypsy and Andalusian singers consider Deep Song to be the superior of the two. Not only does *jondo* represent the most ancient and pure style of singing but also in order to interpret it, the singer requires far greater vocal resources. Indeed, this music calls forth some of the most difficult and exacting vocal techniques, literally tearing sound from the singer's throat.

The Gypsy singers, in contrast to Andalusian *cantaores*, are less bound to the formalities of the various song styles. Where Andalusian singing is characterized by moderation and purity, the Gypsy's is freer in design and more expressive of self rather than conventionalized in form. Because Gypsies project emotions of the moment, one rarely hears their songs repeated exactly alike. Highly responsive to audience encouragement (cries such as "¡Olé!" "¡Anda!"), the Gypsy varies his performances according to mood. Prolonging notes, sliding from one to another through a series of infinite gradations, the Gypsy's singing, like incantation, tends to hypnotize the audience. A nasal, metallic tone is deliberately cultivated, subordinating sweetness of tone to the *duende* (spirit) of the song. To the unaccustomed listener, the music sounds off key.

The problem of classifying the songs is complicated by the fact that some of the great singers transform *cante flamenco* into *jondo* by singing the one in the style of the other. (Unfortunately, the reverse is true also, especially in modern times.) As illustrated in the following anecdote, controversy also exists regarding the degree of difficulty in performing the various songs. In conversation in 1959, Centeno reported that Chacón, the master of *malagueñas* of another generation, held that the *malagueña*, although classified in the flamenco song category, was more difficult to sing than the classic *siguiriya*. "The *siguiriya* has human sorrow built into it, while the singer has to put the pain into the *malagueña*." Actually the *malagueña* incorporates qualities of *jondo*, albeit, as the foregoing indicates, it is not as profound in its basic form unless transformed by a mastersinger. The intensity of emotions as reflected in the facial expressions of *jondo* singers may be seen in the photograph of Manuel Centeno (p. 55), who said, "When you write of our songs, do not forget to say that in them you heard the sound of weeping."

ARTIFACTS

The artifacts used in connection with Deep Song are relatively few in number. In terms of accompaniment, they include principally the guitar, castanets, the tambourine, and the "style stick." Of these four, the tambourine is actually very infrequently used, and most Gypsies, contrary to popular thought, prefer to emulate the sound of the castanets with the snapping of their fingers, called *pitos*, rather than to use the castanets themselves. The "style stick," short, rodlike, and sometimes tipped with iron, is used to rap out the all-important rhythms of the songs, often against a chair rung, although some singers dispense with this in favor of marking the rhythms by drumming their fingers. The "style stick" is most often employed as accompaniment to *siguiriyas gitanas* and to *martinetes.*

In connection with marking rhythms, the *palmas* (hand clapping), and the *zapateos* (the heelwork of the dancers), are also employed for this purpose. With respect to this last point, it should be emphasized that song is the main accompaniment of the dance among the Gypsies, even some of the deepest of *cantes* being danced. Dancers of pure *jondo* styles, such as the widely acclaimed Rosa Durán of Madrid's *Zambra*, are less numerous than flamenco dancers, the far greater degree of sensitivity, artistry, and depth required of the former combining to limit their numbers.

The guitar, while not used as accompaniment to all types of Deep Song, *deblas* and *martinetes* being examples of those sung without guitar accompaniment, stands as the instrument most intimately related to *jondo*. Starkie, in discussing this relationship, noted, "It is the guitarist who creates the atmosphere for the singer and the background which enables him to find scope for his inspiration" (1953:98–99). Because of this intimate relationship, most singers are extremely particular concerning the selection of their guitarist. As expressed by Centeno, "It is important that the guitar player knows the singer and his style." During a private recital it was observed that, at the onset, and at certain intervals, the guitarist thrummed his instrument, seemingly oblivious of his surroundings (the large back room of a tavern engaged by Centeno for exclusive use), while Centeno sat in stony silence, often with his eyes closed. Suddenly, the *soleares, siguiriyas gitanas,* and *martinetes* would burst forth, often overpowering, by sheer force and intensity, the accompaniment which inspired them. And, as noted previously, once vocal expression had been given to the atmosphere created by the guitar, singer and guitarist often seemed to be performing independently of one another.

Constructed at least in part of cypress wood, the guitars of the Gypsy players are usually clamped across the neck to achieve a brilliant as well as metallic tone. Guitarists devote careful attention to these clamps, which are often hand-made and intricately designed. A Gypsy of the Sacro Monte, commenting on the lack of ivory in 1970 for the purpose, worked bits of pearl pajama buttons carefully into the clamp he was in process of carving. The result was a beautiful as well as functional piece of craftsmanship, of which he was inordinately proud. A variety of effects are achieved by striking the guitar strings rather than plucking them, by drumming on the sounding board, and by resorting to the dazzling improvisations which are a part of each player's repertoire, and which place the stamp of individual identity on his work. The accompaniment usually is divided into three parts, the prelude, the theme, and the variations, although, owing to the characteristics of Deep Song, these are all more often *suggestive* than definitive.

For public performances of *jondo* styles, the clothing of the Gypsies is neither as flamboyant nor as calculated to excite audience reaction as is that of flamenco singers and dancers. Instead, clothing worn is generally conservative, assuming a very subsidiary role to the actual songs or dances being performed. In harmony with the themes being expressed, the clothing of male *jondo* stylists is sombre and minor keyed; for example, black suits and white shirts, the latter being devoid of the ruffles and elaborate embroidery favored by flamenco artists. Among the women, the solid-colored traditional *bata de cola* (dress with long train) contrasts with the polka-dotted ruffled prints of their flamenco counterparts.

THE LEARNING AND NATURE OF DEEP SONG

Rooted in the past, traditionally, Deep Song has been handed down from generation to generation within Gypsy culture without benefit of written notation or recourse to formal training. Gypsy informants declared the *jondo* style of singing to be "natural" to them, although, they added, not all Gypsies cultivate it. With Deep Song, as with dancing, Gypsy informants held to the belief that the ability to master the various styles was innate. The only teacher worthy of their note was "experience," that is to say, the hearing and imitating of older singers. In spite of their deeply held belief that only those "born to it" ever completely mastered the *jondo* style, most informants pointed out that *jondo* could be learned by non-Gypsies, provided that they had had intimate and prolonged Gypsy contacts. In essence, the familiar *copla* reported by Brown (1939:132), in which the singer states,

> Although I sing a Gypsy song,
> I'm not a *gitaniyo*. See!
> I lived among them for so long
> That Gypsy singing clung to me.

is an acknowledgment of this last possibility while, at the same time, it succeeds in conveying the impression that the circumstance is unusual.

A traditional folk art, Deep Song's uniqueness has rested in the fact that it is not static, innovations and variations always having been encouraged within limits. This license within a semifixed framework, as it were, has served both to preserve Deep Song's original shape and to maintain its spontaneous quality. As noted by Block, "Gypsies can still achieve by music what it is no longer possible for others in words, the conveying of a thought exactly as it springs into consciousness" (1939:224). As a result of the cultural sanctioning of improvisation within the limits of the various styles, the greatest *jondo* singers have frequently been both composers and poets, many of their improvisations and variations eventually becoming part of the traditional fabric itself.

In an effort to reawaken public interest in Deep Song and to offset the corrupting influences of commercialism, the Deep Song Festival of 1922 was organized by Falla, García Lorca, and other prominent artists and writers of Granada. Limited expressly to nonprofessional singers, contestants were invited to compete for cash prizes in three categories of *cante jondo*, with an additional grand prize added for the best singer of *siguiriyas gitanas*.

> The prize-winner was a man of seventy-three, El Viejo, who walked to Granada from Puente Genil, carrying the same stick he had used at the age of twenty to tap the rhythms.
> "Why did you come?" he was asked.
> "I came to win the prize of a thousand *pesetas* for the best *siguiriya*," he calmly announced. And he did. . . . (Brown 1929:149–150)

In general, it may be accurately stated that *jondo* is sung today almost exclusively by professional or semiprofessional singers. As even a rudimentary listening experience bears out, the variety, number, and quality of vocal resources required to fully and expertly interpret *jondo* are such that only a few singers are ever classified as great masters of the art. Moreover, the use of the term "professional" should not be held to imply that all *jondo* singers are highly paid, that they make their living exclusively by singing, or that their performances are always public. Today the word "professional" designates mainly that the performer is highly skilled in, and recognized for, his art, and that he is in frequent demand for performances whether private or public.

Learning through association and imitation, children in Gypsy culture are encouraged to emulate at a very early age the singing and dancing to which they are exposed all of their lives. Sharing fully, as they do, the adult world, we observed over and over again small children listening to songs, watching the dances being performed by adults, and actually participating in them. On a Málaga wharf, for example, Gypsy children were encountered singing and dancing for sailors lined up on the deck of a docked merchant ship. The eldest girl stated that they were singing *bulerías*, a gay type of flamenco song, in return for which they expected to be rewarded by *pesetas* and candy. She said that she had learned these songs, as well as many others, from hearing her mother and aunts sing them. Asked about Deep Song, she replied proudly, "I am learning to sing in *jondo* style like La Niña de los Peines. One day I shall be just like her." Referring to Deep Song as "true Gypsy song," she pointed out that the songs were "very sad" but told interesting stories and that she and her friends liked the fact that they were sung in connection with weddings and other festive occasions. She concluded her statements with the observation, "We do not sing these songs except among ourselves. Others [referring to non-Gypsies] only like songs full of laughter." A beautiful child, her pride, her maturity, and her demeanor all left the impression of having had a chance encounter with a "Pharaoh's daughter," indeed. She dismissed "court" by gravely accepting some chewing gum.

In summary, all informants interviewed concerning the nature and manner of learning Deep Song stated that it was both traditional and improvised within traditional limits; that it was learned through imitation of and close association with *jondo* singers; that it was part of the experience of children growing up in the culture; and that most of the best singers were "professionals," although they often followed other occupations or trades in addition to that of singing and sang more for private than for public groups. Not only were informants found to be in complete agreement on these four major points but field experiences and observations, coupled with supportive evidence from the literature, upheld their assertions as well.

Meaning of Deep Song

GENERAL MOOD

Defined as "the song of the tragic sense of life," Deep Song is a profoundly expressive, intimate music. Corresponding closely to the moods descriptive of the general musical style termed "Eurasian" by Lomax in his classification of the main musical styles of the world, and under which general term he included the folk music of the south of Spain (1959:935–936), the prevailing and predominant mood of Deep Song is tragic, nostalgic, passionately sad. In addition to these moods, however, Deep Song is expressive also of defiance and human courage. The mood of a typical *soleá*, for example, has been described as "one of sadness, but not of resignation. It is the mood of one who fights against unconquerable odds, but whose soul remains unconquered" (Brown 1929:288). Similarly, the *martinete*, full of descriptions of blood feuds, tribal struggles, and prison, is illustrative of tragedy coupled with human courage.

Violent, tense, impassioned, Deep Song depicts the durability of man, even as he is broken by external and internal forces. In this sense, the sadness and sense of tragedy characteristic of Deep Song cannot be held to be completely devoid of inspiration. Rather, the hopeful expectation which is inherent in many of the songs, primarily that which holds that man's integrity may remain invulnerable even in the face of disaster, is a quality which, in part, explains the durability of this folk art in Andalusian Gypsy culture.

DEEP SONG MOTIFS

In identifying the thematic content of Deep Song, data were obtained from four principal sources: (1) field interviews, (2) private and public performances of Deep Song, (3) recordings, both tape and phonograph, and (4) written primary and secondary sources. Eight motifs, or themes, the terms being used synonymously in this instance, were found to be expressed in the word content of Deep Song: (1) love and loyalty, (2) jealousy, (3) revenge, (4) pride, (5) freedom, (6) persecution of Gypsies, (7) human sorrow, and (8) fatalism and death.

Each motif is treated separately in the sections which follow, in spite of some overlapping between them. Data relative to distinguishing features, informants' responses, and supportive evidence, the last in the form of actual illustrative *coplas*, are given for each. While the selection of the *coplas* was based on their representativeness of the vast body sung, in no way should those included be held to be all inclusive. The collections of Borrow, Brown, Cimorra, Lafuente,

Luna, Starkie, and Quintana yielded the majority of these illustrations, all of which are presented in translated form.

LOVE AND LOYALTY. As reported by all informants interviewed, the motif of love and loyalty was found to constitute a familiar and frequently expressed theme in Deep Song. Subjects included under this general heading concerned mother love, the sorrows of parted lovers, the loyalty of a wife waiting for her husband, and similar references.

As has been noted, the mother motif in Deep Song was found to be expressed in terms of love of children (usually sons) for their mothers rather than the reverse pattern.

Brown, in his collection of songs, reported a *copla* which asked:

> Of all the great misfortunes
> Was ever there another
> As great as mine? Born sightless,
> I've never seen my mother.
> (1929:227)

Many of the songs, generally *martinetes*, were found to be expressions of the grief felt by prisoners as they recalled their mothers and the mother–son relationship. Others, such as this one from the group sung in private by Centeno, reflect the all-encompassing nature of the love of the Gypsy for his mother:

> A cent I gave a blind beggar,
> He blessed my mother.
> What recompense!
> For such a small gift.
> Quintana 1960:190

Relative to songs expressive of passionate love, it was noted that these songs centered more on unrequited love, or on the trials and sorrows of lovers, than on the more positive aspects of love and loyalty. Characterized both by hope and despair, they tended to be sad songs, picturing men and women clinging to illusions and memories, often subordinating their own happiness to that of their loved ones. One contributed by Centeno stated:

> I became marble
> When I heard you were to marry.
> But I wish you well.
> Quintana 1960:191

By way of contrast, however, *coplas* dealing with the subject of infidelity, and penalties for trafficking lightly in love, also were included under this general motif.

Apropos the general theme of love, Torner noted, "In *cante jondo* we do not find any vestiges of religious sentiments but only very human passions—almost exclusively those of love with all of its joys and pains carried to the maximum sentimental exaltation" (1944:II, 41). Cimorra, too, accorded love a prominent position in the thematic content of Deep Song, pointing out that it was "*el amor difícil, el amor contrariado, on una palabra, las tribulaciones del querer*" (the tribulations of love) (1943:91).

JEALOUSY. Starkie, in discussing *siguiriyas gitanas*, noted that "they were all passionately sad songs describing jealous love, hunger, gaol, death, and there was hardly one that did not bring in the *maresita vieja* [old mother] or the *puñalá* [dagger-thrust]" (1935:438). There is a *copla* particularly illustrative of Starkie's observation, which chillingly states:

> I killed her. She belonged to me.
> I killed the woman that I loved.
> And should she come to life, I know
> A hundred times I'd kill her so
> She'd ne'er deceive me here below.
> Brown 1929:207

The jealousy motif appears to dominate in public performances of *jondo* styles. This is apparent most where dance accompanies the song, the dancers' exaggerated gestures frequently and forcefully underlining the sexual tensions occasioned by male/female rejection and jealousy. Lomax, in his study of Andalusian styles, made a similar observation stating,

> The whole area is dominated by hunger and, beneath a surface gaiety, an underlying asceticism and melancholy and a mood of violence and sexual jealousy exist—all brilliantly expressed in a neo-Eurasian musical art, in which dance and song are inextricably linked (1959:935–936).

REVENGE. Identified as a Deep Song motif by half of all informants interviewed, the theme of Gypsy revenge has occupied a prominent place in literature pertaining to Gypsy law and to Gypsy music. Reference to this type of *copla*, dealing with tribal revenge, has already been made in Chapter 3 in the section dealing with the preeminence of Gypsy law. Of the two presented here, one refers to personal revenge:

> I sallied forth upon my grey,
> With him my hated foe,
> And when we reached the narrow way
> I dealt a dagger blow.
> Borrow 1908:293

The other is more generalized in its warning:

> Today, since I'm the anvil,
> I know I must forbear . . .
> If ever I'm the hammer,
> Beware, my friend, beware.
> Brown 1929:153

In general, *coplas* dealing with revenge are seldom sung in public, being confined mainly to private Deep Song sessions where audiences are constituted exclusively of Gypsies. Frequent allusions to Gypsy justice, and numerous Gypsy maledictions, were noted. These, in the main, however, were concerned with the revenge of men and women rejected in love, or betrayed by friends. Phrases such as "beware if our paths should cross," and curses dealing with painful deaths or afflictions, were noted as being the most common types of warnings and imprecations expressed in the songs.

PRIDE. The pride of the Gypsy was found to be manifested in a number of the *coplas* reported in the literature and recorded in actual performance. Concerning this motif, more than half of the informants interviewed independently identified it as operable in Deep Song. A favorite *copla* which treats of this theme states:

> Gypsies don't deny in shame
>   The race from which they all descend:
> I don't claim that we're the same,
>   And yet you still can be my friend.
>   Brown 1929:159.

Despite its age, this *copla*, as well as those emphasizing Gypsy "royal blood" and the rejection of non-Gypsy life ways, is among the *coplas* most frequently sung in public with variations and modifications dictated by the particular singer's *estilo* (style). While pride in "race" is evinced in the *copla* quoted, it is unique in that it is one of the few in which the non-Gypsy is accorded friendship status.

FREEDOM. As is the case with traditional themes in Gypsy culture, the motif of freedom was declared by a large majority of informants to be glorified through the word content of Deep Song. María Amaya, interviewed in 1959 in Granada's Sacro Monte on her seventy-fourth birthday, stated, "Freedom, the thing most prized by the Gypsy, is one of the things he most sings of in *cante jondo*." She illustrated her assertion by singing a *copla* in which the following lament was heard:

> Others ask for riches
>   While I, dying—ask only for liberty.
> But my father
>   You do not give it to me.

The value placed by the Gypsies on freedom has found a variety of expression in the songs. By way of example, the so-called prison songs, usually *martinetes* or *deblas*, were noted to contain innumerable tragic lamentations concerning the loss of freedom; often freedom was found being compared to other things, the value placed upon it always being greater than that of material possessions; and, not infrequently, it was manifested in declarations of friendship and love. The following *copla* from the Brown collection is illustrative of these various emphases:

> I'm going to sell my clothes.
>   Who'll buy my clothes from me?
> I'll sell them for a song
>   To get you free.
>   (1929:171)

PERSECUTION OF GYPSIES. *Coplas* which tell of the persecution of Gypsies continue to occupy a prominent position in Deep Song. Observed to be less frequently sung in public than those which treat of the more abstract forms of human suffering, these songs were found to be rooted in an historical past in which violence and cruelty were not uncommonly sanctioned by law. Numerically weak, and often the victims of brutality, the Gypsy in Spain expressed his grief, his frustration, and his unconquerable will in his songs of persecution. The power of these songs, many of which have survived for centuries, has been said to have inspired the *Gypsy Ballads* of García Lorca. So successful was Lorca in capturing the spirit of Gypsy persecution, as the following excerpts from his work may serve to illustrate, that Gypsy informants throughout Andalusia, most of them illiterate, referred over and over again to Lorca's ballad of the Civil Guard in illustrating this motif, adding that the words were often sung in *jondo* style:

> Their deadly faces are leaden,
> Therefore they never weep:
> Hearts of patent-leather,
> They come along the road.
>
> . . . . .
>
> Through the shadowy streets
> The Gypsy old women flee
>
> . . . . .
>
> Rosa de los Camborios
> Sobs on the step of her door
> With both breasts cut away
> And placed on a serving tray.
>
> . . . . .
>
> O city of the Gypsies!
> Flames encircle the town;
> Through a tunnel of silence
> The Civil Guard departs.
>
> Humphries 1954:49–52

Most informants interviewed identified the persecution motif as being frequently expressed through Deep Song. Of actual Gypsy *coplas* illustrative of the theme, the following are representative of the many sung:

> We are poor Gypsies
> Poorer than larks
> Spaniards and guards
> Deny us even the shade.
>
> Luna 1942:65

> And as I o'er the water rode
> A man came suddenly;
> And he his love and kindness showed
> By setting his dog on me.
>
> Borrow 1908:295

> I for a cup of water cried,
> But they refus'd my prayer,
> Then straight to the road I hied,
> And fell to robbing there.
>
> Borrow 1908:294

The third of the *coplas*, a rationalization for antisocial behavior, reinforces the observation that earlier forms of persecution in Spain operated only to intensify Gypsy activities of this nature.

HUMAN SORROW.   The essence of *jondo*, as noted previously, is the tragic sense of life. Through song, as the following *copla* illustrates, the Gypsy has been said to have both glorified and found relief from sorrow:

> A captive in a prison cell,
> I sing the woes I feel,
> For thus I file away my chains,
> My chains of heavy steel.
> Brown 1929:144

All informants interviewed identified the motif of human sorrow as part of Deep Song, noting that sorrow constituted the theme most frequently expressed both in public and in private Deep Song performances. It was pointed out by Starkie (1937:289–290) that some of the most beautiful *coplas*, usually sung as *siguiriyas* or *soleares*, were illustrative of this theme:

> Every day before the world
> I weep for my sorrows;
> And everyone feels pity in his heart
> for my sad fate.

> Into the fields alone I go
> to cry out my woe.
> As my soul is full of
> sorrows, alone I go.

A *copla* sung by Centeno simply stated:

> I am drunk
> If you knew why,
> You would be, too.

Relative to the theme of sorrow, Centeno, related a conversation between Chacón and Manuel Torres in which Chacón is reported to have said, "I sing better than you, but I will die with the pain of knowing that I do not have the feeling for expressing human sorrow that is yours. You only shout, but it breaks my heart" (Quintana 1960:203).

FATALISM AND DEATH. In all instances the death theme in Deep Song was coupled by informants with Gypsy fatalism. Fatalism and death were identified as motifs held to be in a thematic category apart from that which dealt with generalized human suffering. Cimorra, in a section of his work devoted entirely to this subject, stated, "A theme frequently seen in Deep Song is the obsession, the fear, the finality of death" (1943:97). He attributed the fatalism of the people of Andalusia to "oriental influences," observing that they gave articulation to their preoccupation with the mysteries of life and death through *cante jondo*. By way of illustrating the philosophical tone of many of the *coplas* sung, he included the following in his selection:

> There is no greater truth in this world
> Than that of a deep grave;
> There money is ended,
> power and beauty
> and the cloak of nobility.

A *copla* sung by a Gypsy informant in Granada was very similar to the one reported by Cimorra. It stated:

Visit the cemetery
If you wish.
There's where the sad lessons of life stop.

Starkie, referring to García Lorca's work *Poema del Cante Jondo*, observed that in the poems, a stylization of Andalusian Gypsy song, "The tragic *siguiriya* and the mournful *soleá* turn our thoughts to death" (1953:107–108).

Asked for brief, descriptive concluding statements concerning the meaning of Deep Song, all informants stated that it was intimate, personal, and sentimental and that, in the main, it dealt with human suffering—the round of life and death.

Use of Deep Song

The occasions and conditions under which Deep Song is sung in Andalusian Gypsy culture constitute two separate categories. The first, dealing with both public and private performances, embraces those aspects of Deep Song performances which may be generally, although not exclusively, designated as "entertainment," while the second is confined to performances associated in Gypsy culture with the life crises.

ENTERTAINMENT

To understand the use of Deep Song in connection with either public professional entertainment or private celebrations, it is necessary to bear in mind a point made earlier in this book, that is, the tendency of Gypsies to "rejoice in being sad." This paradox of joy and sadness traditionally has been reflected in Deep Song performances, where the songs of the "tragic sense of life" have occupied a prominent role in celebrations and entertainments of a wide variety of types.

Questioned regarding the occasions and conditions under which Deep Song is sung, one informant pointed out that "for *jondo* to be genuine, the singer has to want to sing, and has to feel his audience's response to him. For that reason, it is an intimate music, which is best heard in small, private groups." One great singer (seventy-six years old) explained his reluctance to sing publicly in the following terms:

I sing when I feel like it. Not for money. I feel like singing for you not because you are intelligent, but because you can *feel* the song. I saw that I could sing for you. I sing for few people today.

While his attitude does not hold true for all *jondo* singers, it was noted that even those paid performers who sang regularly at public cafes, restaurants, and hotels performed best after the major part of their audiences had left and only small audiences of "*cabales*" ("those who understand") remained.

Sung in theaters, cafes, hotels, and at private parties, Deep Song is also heard during the fairs, fiestas, and religious festivals held throughout Andalusia. At private Gypsy *juergas*, which are given at any time and for any reason (or for no apparent reason at all!) Deep Song accompanied by the dance, or, as expressed by María Amaya, "listened to in deepest silence like a mass," was reported to play a principal role. However, of far, far greater importance, according to Gypsy informants, was the role of Deep Song in the life crises.

THE LIFE CRISES

Relative to the life crises, Deep Song was found to be used in connection with those of birth and marriage, with all Gypsy informants interviewed attesting to the fact that *cante jondo* is customarily heard at private Gypsy ceremonies and celebrations connected with these two events. Aside from maintaining that Deep Song was the natural culmination of Gypsy baptisms and weddings, informants stated that some of the songs contained "magical" properties which insured good fortune for the new child, or for the newly married couple. Of greatest importance in celebrations honoring Gypsy weddings, the song of virginity was held to symbolize, as it has done for centuries, the purity of the bride. In addition, numerous Deep Song *coplas* were recorded which reinforced Gypsy laws and traditions pertaining to conjugal fidelity, and which underlined marital responsibilities.

Only a small number of Gypsies cited the use of Deep Song in association with the life crisis of death. They asserted that through the songs, the living expressed their grief, and the departure of the spirits of the dead was facilitated. Non-Gypsy informants supported the contention that Deep Song was sung at Gypsy wakes, but, in the main, it was not possible to validate this data in the field to any appreciable extent. Stated one, "The Gypsies will never admit that they sing at their wakes, but they do. It is then that one hears the purest *jondo*. Outsiders are never admitted as they are to Gypsy weddings."

All informants reported that Deep Song was heard at festivities celebrating the good fortune of an individual or family, provided that the services of a good *cantaor* were available.

Function of Deep Song

As seen in Gypsy culture, the purposes of Deep Song embrace both personal and ethnic considerations. Under the former, Deep Song was said to be used for the singer's own consolation, that is, to relieve his personal feelings of grief and self-pity, to reinforce his sense of pride, courage, and innate dignity, and, lastly, as in the case of the better "professional" singers, to provide him with a culturally accepted means of earning part or all of his livelihood. Principally, however, as reported more than forty years ago by Brown, "A Gypsy always sings for himself first of all. He sings and dances to relieve his feelings" (1929:77).

In 1968 we recorded the thoughts and feelings of a well-known Gypsy singer, a woman who, suffering from a serious throat affliction, said, "*It is my curse to sing.*" She spoke as follows:

We are "born" with all this—you have only to look at me. . . . I am told that
it is my curse to sing. The doctors everywhere tell me to stop singing. But I forget—even those terrible operations that they have to perform on me—and continue singing.

I don't sing like some people for the money—but I sing because when I hear
the guitar, my heart is filled with the desire to sing—and I cannot hold it back.
I sing because I carry it in my soul. . . . And I don't remember that it makes
me sick.

Then, when I get sick, I say "Oh God, I will never sing again in my life."
. . . And I sometimes think I won't even be able to speak again. . . . My husband
says to me "Don't sing—if you sing I am going to kill you! What are you
thinking of—to make yourself sick—to spend everything we have on doctors
and medicine?"—and I say to him, "I swear I will not sing again."

It is always the same. It is a terrible shame, because my song is from the heart.
. . . It is *true song* . . . and it fills me with rage to have to turn over the singing
to others who do not sing as well as I. . . . I cannot tell them that it is not
good . . . sometimes they do it all right . . . but they do not *feel* it. . . .
Even so, I have to say, "¡*Olé*!" But the tears often flow down my face from the
frustrations and nervousness that this has given me. . . . Crying so that the
tears fall . . . *Me*! Imagine.

And I say, "*Madre mía, why* do I have this throat?" I would give anything
not to get hoarse. . . . Not for the money because I have enough of that—but
rather for that joy [*alegría*]. For example, not too many days ago, my husband
met a friend and they went out to drink a few *copitas* [little cups of sherry]
. . . but very much later—during the night—I was sleeping and I heard music
through the door. I got up and said, "Who is it?" And it was my husband and
a group seated at the table. And they had food and drink, and each one sang.
. . . It was a very pleasing "ambience." Each one would sing—and they would
look at me. They would ask me, "Couldn't you just sing one little *copla*?" And
I wanted to, but my husband said "No, don't force yourself."

And I suffered more that night than as if they had killed me. Because I
could not sing. And my husband felt very bad to see me like that. . . . I carried
such a weight!

Regarding ethnic considerations, Deep Song was viewed as serving to inculcate cultural values, and to communicate cultural goals and understandings. In
addition, under certain circumstances, some of the songs were considered to contain magical properties, that is to say, to bring good or bad "luck," and, as in
the minority of instances just reported, to facilitate the departure of the spirits of
the dead.

Values said by all Gypsy informants to be communicated by the songs
included those pertinent to mother love and to marital fidelity. In addition, informants stated that by illustrating the inescapability of "fate," the songs taught
the acceptance of the joys and sorrows of life. All informants pointed out that
not only the word content but also the manner of singing the songs, the occasions
at which they were sung, and the "old age" of the songs clearly delineated their
cultural importance.

Regarding the communication of cultural goals and understandings, the
songs were held to reinforce demands for familial and ethnic loyalty, pride, and
solidarity and to illustrate the penalties and sufferings occasioned by their denial.
Songs dealing with the persecution of the Gypsies were cited in twenty instances

as being expressive both of the need for ethnic solidarity and of Gypsy durability, while those pertaining to Gypsy revenge were cited by fourteen informants in support of their assertions that the songs taught "obedience to the Gypsy way."

Cultural Regard for Deep Song

Pertinent to the general cultural regard for Deep Song, three questions were asked of all Gypsy informants interviewed: (1) Does Deep Song fulfill its purposes? (2) Is Deep Song regarded as an enculturative vehicle? (3) Is Deep Song valued over and above its practical applications? All questions were phrased in suitable terminology so that, for example, the second question was most commonly phrased as, "Does Deep Song help children to learn the Gypsy way of life?"

All Gypsy informants responded in the affirmative to all three questions, although significant qualifications were made concerning each. Informants variously expressed opinions that Deep Song was in danger of disappearing and that the best of *jondo* was being less frequently heard. Outside materialistic interests were viewed by some as conflicting with cultural interests, while others held that the greater independence of the younger generation had the effect of weakening the "teachings" of the songs. The fatalistic motif in Deep Song was regarded by a minority of informants as meaningful only for *los viejos* (the aged).

Concerning the third question, informants pointed principally to personal and esthetic satisfactions in support of their opinions that Deep Song had value which transcended its practical applications. Two, both professional entertainers, maintained that things which had no materialistic value did not "live long." Consequently, they said, it was a good thing that Deep Song had both.

The comparison of Deep Song motifs to the traditional cultural themes transmitted by Andalusian Gypsies, revealed themes common to both sets of data. For example, the prominence accorded the theme of freedom was noted to have found a variety of expression in Deep Song, while the belief of Gypsies in their ethnic superiority was reflected clearly in the many songs expressive of Gypsy pride and durability. Regarding the theme of Gypsy loyalty, concern with filial devotion and marital fidelity was evinced in numerous *coplas*. In addition, songs in which the motif of jealousy was present served to reinforce demands for absolute loyalty in situations involving even passionate emotion. Motifs of revenge, in songs dealing with the inescapability of tribal justice, corresponded closely to similar aspects embraced by the theme of the preeminence of Gypsy law. Although Gypsy fatalism was the theme about which least outright validation was recorded, it proved to be one of the most dominant in Deep Song.

While less frequently heard in pure form, and less important today as an enculturative vehicle than in the past, Deep Song continues to echo and perpetuate the thematic content of Andalusian Gypsy culture. "For us," said an elderly informant, "the Great Song, like tears, always will be a part of our lives, and of our sorrows." His confidence in the durability of this ancient art form has been supported by almost all Gypsies with whom we have had prolonged contact in the decade since past. In 1970 we continued to hear accounts of the Deep Song Festival of 1922, almost a half-century later, from both young and old Gypsies. A festival we attended in 1968 duplicated the moonlight setting of the original, at the foot of the Alhambra, and was attended by some of the best *cantaores* (folksingers) of southern Spain. But the wistful desire for the days of Falla and García Lorca whispered through that Granada night, still recalling days "when the *cante* was truly pure."

5

The Gypsy "Way"

AS WE HAVE NOTED, the *ethos* of Andalusian Gypsy culture was character-ized by extreme forms of conservatism which addressed themselves to the preservation and perpetuation of its traditional themes and life ways. A distinguishing feature of the culture as a whole was its highly developed abil-ity to select from the outside world those features which could be easily inte-grated into the existing cultural framework without disturbing its basic structure. Much in the same way that the addition of ornate facades to some of the cave entrances in the Sacro Monte failed to alter the interior physical organization of the homes, so, too, the Gypsy took and used ideas and artifacts from other cul-tures without changing his fundamental value systems. In a classic among Gypsy essays, Symons wrote of the Gypsies that

> the world has no power over them. They live by rote and by faith and by tra-dition, . . . they go about in our midst reading our secrets, knowing more about us than we do about ourselves. . . . They make theirs whatever is of use to them; they reject whatever their instinct forbids them to take (Sampson 1930:4).

Gypsy Catholicism

Grellmann, one of the first to comment extensively on the fact that Gypsies in the eighteenth and nineteenth centuries regulated themselves in religious mat-ters according to the country where they lived, stated in his famous dissertation (1807:79–81),

> No Gypsy has an idea of submission to any fixed profession of faith; it is as easy for him to change his religion at every new village, as for another person to shift his coat. They suffer themselves to be baptized in Christian countries; among the Mahometans to be circumcised.

The old adage quoted by Grellmann, "The Gypsy's church was built with bacon, and the dogs ate it," is challenged today by Clébert, who notes that among contemporary Gypsies,

> What counts is the evidence of an intense religious faith outside of any relig-ious persuasion. Whether they are Christians or Mussulmans (or even though they may be outside of every "official" credo) the great majority of Gypsies give proof of a strength and enthusiasm in matters of faith which astonish even priests (1963:133–134).

An informant in Malaga recently stated that Spanish Catholicism, with its emphasis on the sufferings of Christ, was in many ways consistent with the pre-occupation of Gypsies with death and pain. As a consequence of this emotional tone, she advanced the theory that the Gypsy in Andalusia found within the church an extension of his own tendency to relate the sorrows of the past to the present. In a like vein, the teachings of the Catholic Church regarding fidelity in marriage, and the obligation of marital partners to beget children, were found to be in accord with Gypsy values, as was the appeal of the elaborate and beautiful church rituals, accompanied as they were by music and dancing.

Of far greater significance than any of these factors, however, is the fact that the traditional monotheism of Gypsies, and their own mythologies, are compatible with Christianity. The efforts of Catholic priests who have utilized Gypsy beliefs in working with them has facilitated their accommodation to Catholicism. For example, Gypsy allegiance to the Church has been strengthened by its recognition of La Macarena, patron saint of Andalusian Gypsies, and its support of the annual Gypsy pilgrimage to Sainte-Marie-de-la-Mer, France, in homage to Sara, the legendary Gypsy Black Virgin.

Physically visible in the form of Catholic photographs, religious medals, plaques, and statuary, the sedentary Gypsies with whom we have worked exhibit pride in these displays of faith. They have been engaged by Granada's city councils for three centuries for the traditional dances in the annual Corpus Christi processions, the role of dance as an art form suitable for religious ritual being recognized by the Church in Spain. Performing Gypsies are much sought after also by the many religious societies, occupational groups, and clubs which erect *casetas* (temporary buildings within which exclusive entertainments are presented and refreshments served during the ten-day celebration following Corpus Christi), and competition is keen among them to acquire the services of the best of the Gypsy dancers, guitarists, and singers. Characterized by blocks of candy booths, carnival games, and rides, the Corpus Christi celebration continues early into the morning hours, with noisy crowds of people in constant motion and interaction. One of our Gypsy informants, who accepted an invitation to dance in the private *caseta* of the *Guardia Civil*, the traditional enemy of Spain's Gypsies, told us that she did not go down to the *feria* grounds often because "too many common people mingle there, and its religious meaning is weakened by the excesses."

The presence of contradictions, overlapping dogmas, and superstition in the religious expression of Andalusian Gypsies should not be overinterpreted as a lack of sincerity or as just another example of Gypsy opportunism. Erratic attendance at Mass, runaway marriage by poorer Gypsies without benefit of civil or religious sanction, and their limited understanding of Church sacraments may all be cited as illustrative of the "superficiality" of Gypsy Catholicism. In spite of the truth of these observations, baptism is accepted by virtually all sedentary Gypsies today, and there is a decided trend among them, which will be discussed in a later chapter, toward fuller acceptance of and participation in the religious life of Spain. They take the names of the saints and celebrate, as do Spaniards, their particular saint's day. The fact is that in religious matters the Gypsies have exercised the same selectivity which has marked their life style down through the centuries. It is significant also that while in their religious observances and interpretations Gypsies exhibit a wider range of variability than is apparent among other Spaniards, the individuality which characterizes aspects of Spanish Catholicism is not limited to Gypsies solely in Spain. Its counterparts may be found among Spaniards of differing social class and economic and educational backgrounds. Indeed, one informant noted that it is the freedom to exercise choice within a rigidly fixed religious framework that attracts Gypsies to the Church. While this may not be representative of idealized Catholicism, it nevertheless is operative in the reality world of its Gypsy communicants.

By Rote, by Faith, by Tradition

As first recorded in 1959, Gypsy conservatism was especially pronounced in the degree and kind of prestige accorded to the aged in Gypsy society, wisdom and power being highly correlated by Gypsies with age. Although contemporary Andalusian Gypsies recognize Spanish law, there remain vestiges of the older system of the chieftainship in their society. Internal political organization is based on family households which unite to form tribal groups, each of which elects its own chief. Elected chiefs, erroneously referred to in romantic literature as "kings," are characteristically older men known for strength, courage, wisdom, and ability to administer Gypsy justice impartially. Along with the respect paid to the chiefs, particularly striking in the past was Gypsy regard for the "old tribal mother" (*phuri dai*), who traditionally acted as guardian of ancient moral codes. She ruled over women and children and, in cooperation with the chief, occasionally even taking his place should he have been absent at a critical moment. In describing the typical *phuri dai*, Block wrote,

> Her age is awe-inspiring. Her cry "*seom phuri, seom phuri!*" (I am old, I am old!), arouses not only the respect of her fellow tribesmen, but also the pity and terror of the non-Gypsy population. No one dares to laugh at her shrunken figure or her ugly face. Her piercing gaze strikes anyone in her immediate neighborhood dumb. They are afraid of her; there is a feeling that a wish from her might bring ill luck (1939:170–171).

The increased dependence of Granada's sedentary Gypsies on civil justice has tended to mask the traditional role of the secret Gypsy tribunals (the *Kris*) to which reference was made in Chapter 3. "Well protected from any contacts with non-Gypsy culture and society, the *kris* [is] capable of maintaining itself over long periods of relative disuse. . ." (Gropper 1967:1055). Tribunals of older men continue to pass judgment on matters pertaining to tribal disputes, violations of Gypsy law, financial grievances, insults, and so forth. The advice of senior women may be sought, although their presence at such meetings is not, to the best of our knowledge, ever tolerated. The singling out of one *phuri dai* is no longer overtly apparent among Sacro Monte Gypsies. However, the privileges and deference accorded older women who demonstrate characteristics similar to those of the male chiefs underscore the high cultural regard in which they still are held.

In addition to the respect accorded the aged, the family continues to form the basis of Gypsy society, with kinship feelings extending outward into the society, that is, far beyond immediate kin. Although the father serves as head of the family, aspects of the matriarchate continue to be manifest among Granada's Gypsies. Matriarchal tendencies were described both as being the result of the economic importance of women in the support of the home and as remnants of the former widespread Gypsy practice of tracing descent through the mother. Even in 1970, some traces of this practice remained, but these, together with other structural changes, particularly centering on place of residence, appeared to be in a state of transition and were difficult to delineate clearly.

The noted outward extension of kinship feelings was held by the Gypsies to account for the fact that any shame or misfortune which befell any one member of their tribe was considered to reflect upon them all. Similarly, it was pointed out by informants that the responsibility to avenge individual wrongs and injuries was shared not only by the individual's immediate kin but by the group as a whole as well. This attitude was, in fact, very little different from the situation as described by Bercovici some forty years ago:

> The *gitanerías* of Seville, Granada, Córdoba, and Madrid are the reservoirs of the Gypsydom of Spain. Each Gypsy or family of Gypsies belongs to a *gitanería*. The old authority of the Gypsy chief still holds sway over the members of his tribe, the laws of the country notwithstanding. The racial memory of an organization keeps Gypsies together as a body. Though a Gypsy knows he cannot depend, when in trouble with the civil or criminal authorities, upon the whole Gypsydom of Spain, he knows that the *Triana* or the *Albaicín* [Sacro Monte] will come to his rescue—will indeed impoverish itself to save him from a prison sentence, or rescue him from the gallows (1928:141–142).

In summary, as Clébert has reiterated,

> The essential nucleus of the Gypsy organization is the family. Authority is held there by the father who, in the family, plays a role similar to that of the tribal chief. As for the woman [senior] on the family scale, she is the *phuri dai*: her power is unofficial and occult, but it is often of solid and of immediate reality (1963:128–129).

"That's Why We Are Gypsies"

Among the Fajardo-Maya Gypsies of the Sacro Monte, the family includes Joaquín the father (*"el que manda"*—"he who orders"); his wife Carmen; their oldest daughter Isabel; her husband Pepe, a non-Gypsy, (who, according to Gypsy custom, settled in the locality of Isabel's parents); their daughter Carmela; and, more recently, her husband Juan and small sons, Juanito and Pepito. In addition, the family over which Joaquín dominates includes a son, Antonio; a younger daughter, María; María's husband; her son Pepito, and various cousins, elderly relatives, and other grandchildren. Although each nuclear family occupies its own dwelling, the close proximity of their caves sustains a uxorilocal-like residence pattern which only recently has shown a tendency toward change. In spite of failing health, Joaquín's authority embraces the entire family and extends over

Los mayores

Fajardo-Maya Gypsies
of the Sacro Monte

Isabel

María

all households. As chief, he is consulted in matters regarding commitment of funds, relationships with non-Gypsies, and any important decisions affecting individual and group welfare. His word is regarded as absolute, albeit it tends to be modified somewhat by his own keen awareness of acculturative forces currently at work in the culture.

LA CAPITANA

Contrary to expectations, Isabel, Joaquín's eldest daughter, not his wife, functions as the family's dominant female. A handsome woman, forty-seven-years old, Isabel serves as daughter, wife, mother, sister, grandmother, and as *la capitana* (the "Captain") of the family's main business, its touristically oriented *zambras*. Her daily life consists of an almost never-ending round of activities: overseeing the housekeeping of her own five-room cave complex—"If ever they carry Pepe in dead, they will see our bed made, clean and white"; cooking large midday meals, usually for a group of relatives; going down to the town "with a flower in my hair for dignity"; and by 5 P.M., ordering, directing, and performing herself in the *zambra*. Performances usually continue into the evening, and it is typical for Isabel's "day" to end at 1 A.M. and start again six hours later. Although Isabel carries the main responsibility for engaging performers—singers, dancers, guitarists—attracting tour groups to the *cuevas* (of which three are utilized only for *zambra* performances), and maintaining group discipline, including the settling of frequent disputes, rivalries, and feuds, she disclaims the fact that she is the actual leader of the family *zambra*. Asked if she became *la capitana* as her parents grew older, she replied,

> No. But because I am the oldest. . . . My mother only had two daughters. I, the oldest, have not only my art but also an ability to be with people. (My sister is always under contract, traveling all over Spain and outside of Spain.) So, as my mother grew older, she said, "Isabel, you put yourself at the center of the business," . . . and that is where I am—in the foreground . . . where I'll probably be until I die. . . . But I am *not* the "captain." The captain is my father. . . . But I am the one who appears to be in the foreground because my parents like to sit in the doorway of the cave used for the *zambra* . . . in the fresh air, eating an ice cream . . . and they don't have to feel obligated to be inside all the time.

The Gypsy "way," as reflected in Isabel's self-portrait in words, centered primarily on involvement in acceptable occupation activities (for example, the *zambra*), attitudes toward parents, and distinctions made between *gitanos* and *payos*. Other of the culture's traditional themes manifested themselves in her life history recountings, starting with her earliest recollections of going to work at age seven.

"MY LIFE AND HEALTH ARE STUCK TO THE WALLS"

I started to work in the *zambra* at the end of the Sacro Monte road. I was seven years old and wanted very much to dance. What *alegría* to dance every day —to become a great artist! In those days there were only two *zambras*; not as many as there are now [six]. And I started to sing because my father played the guitar at home and I was just always singing. I worked for that man, and because in time I could do everything *very* well (everyone in the world agreed!), there were Gypsies who were very jealous of me. Naturally, when I would come out to dance and the people would like it, they turned against me. We would have fights [physical] and, finally, the mothers started to fight.

But my mother had a little cave, not like it is today. We lived in it. It was said to my mother, "With the artistic talents of your family you do not need to be exploited by anyone. You, with this cave which is a treasure, in the middle of the Sacro Monte Road [that is, an ideal location where visitors stop], why don't you mount the dance right here in your home?" Finally the moment came when we started. We took one of the rooms of the cave and made it into a *sala de fiesta* where we performed in the evenings. The other room was my mother and father's bedroom. At night, after the dance, we would move the children's beds back into the salon, so that they could sleep.

The three of us were very young; (my mother, my sister María, and I) and handsome, and we would fix ourselves and sit in the doorway of the cave. And then, when a car came, we would say, "Come see the dance, young men,"—and upon seeing us, young, made-up, and very well combed, they took notice of us.

(The ability of Gypsy women to project their physical and sexual force in the service of their commercial interests—that is, to attract potential *zambra* or fortune-telling clients—has been elevated by them to a virtual art form. Disgruntled male customers, who respond to the lure only to find its promise never consummated in fact, continue to complain bitterly of having been "taken in" by them, a complaint more reflective of their own motives than those of Gypsies.)

My sister was very young and my brother, too, but I was very much in the foreground—"*muy simpática*,"—the prinicipal dancer and singer. My father played the guitar, and later, my husband learned to play the tambourine, and my little girl performed, too, because we all have it in our *blood* and, therefore, know how to dance. And, so, the family formed the *cuadro*—and the people came, more than we could accommodate—and so God helped us. And jealousy flowed from one cave to the other. . . . Over time we prospered, took over still another cave and another, enlarged them, and that is the way it went. And the *dueña* of that other *zambra* said, "Look, they have taken away the business." That is why it is, even today, they are still jealous.

So, I have worked since I was very little, as have my husband and daughter. Every night we do not stop. Therefore, if someone has a little more than someone else, it is because of that. *I have left my life and health stuck to the walls by working so hard.* That's the way it is. As you know my parents have worked very hard. They have been very good to us. My father ran one *zambra*, my mother was in the next cave, and I ran the third. That way we have made our living. Then came the war [Spanish Civil War] and things were much harder, no? And then I got married—when I was very very young—and gave birth to my daughter. Now I am forty-seven years old, but, *nadie me ha mojado la oreja todavía* [no one has wet my ear yet—that is, taken advantage of me]—and still I dance and sing. Eh?

In violation of Gypsy law, Isabel married a non-Gypsy, Pepe, a marriage which did not result in her tribal exclusion nor in the loss of lineage. She described her first meeting with Pepe, thirty-three years ago, when she was fourteen years old.

"HE CAST HIS EYE UPON ME"

It was the day of Saint Cecilia and, as it was the custom, everyone came up to the Sacro Monte to see the sacred caves [catacombs]. Afterwards, we *gitanas* started to jump rope in the little plaza below, and some boys came from the

Albaicín whom we did not know. Finally, one of them cast his eye upon me and asked, "Do you want me to turn the rope?" I liked him, and he began speaking the words of a *novio*. I waited for him the next day, but he did not come. And I said to my friend, "Be careful of the boy [Pepe] from yesterday."

A year later—a year later—yes, a year later he passed through our *barrio* with another girl friend, a little girl like me but not a Gypsy. And he was seen by friends of mine to whom he spoke *piropos* [compliments spoken aloud by boys to girls during the *paseo*] . . . . And when they told me they had seen him, I said, "¡*Claro*! [Naturally!] he is here looking for me. The moment he sees me all will be finished with that other girl." . . . I went into the street pretending that I did not know he was there. Don't you think that was a good idea? Now you'll see. . . . And so I went out, well dressed, presenting myself with style. And upon seeing me—he was struck dumb! Frozen! Pow! . . . Then we started to like one another a lot. He heard me sing, and we made *fiestas*, and became *novios*—he a *payo* and I a *gitana*—and my parents were not aware. We went together that way for a year, and after that, we went off, Gypsy style [eloped]—the two of us.

Asked about family reactions to their elopement, Isabel avoided those of her own family and dwelt instead upon Pepe's parents. In part, this reflected her own loyalties, but, more importantly, the respect with which all Sacro Monte Gypsies have come to regard Pepe in the nearly three decades of his life with them. The key role Isabel played in the *zambra* by the time of her marriage, and public recognition of her outstanding talents as a young performer, also served to reduce group hostilities directed at them. "Anyway, all that is past now."

Aside from Pepe's acceptance of the terms under which a *payo* might live among Gypsies, the prewar acceleration of Gypsy and Andalusian acculturation, especially as related to the flamenco arts, was carried over into the chaotic years immediately following the war's end. Over time, Pepe, in a sense more Gypsy than the Gypsies with whom he has lived his entire adult life, has demonstrated a generosity and kindness toward Granada's poorer Gypsies to which even rival groups pay homage. His concern for them and his insights regarding changing aspects of their culture are examined through his own words, in a later section of this book. Speaking of Pepe's family, Isabel noted,

> *Luck came out on my side.* . . . At first they said to Pepe, "to go off with a Gypsy—this and that" . . . but then some one who knew my parents all of their lives said, "But the Gypsy with whom your son has eloped is a marvelous Gypsy from a very good family—a very rare type of family." And then his family saw me, very proper, no? . . . and we were married in the church. . . . Pepe's mother became closer to me than anyone else. She spent many days with me [actually, she means years] . . . . *What is amazing about this is that I was a Gypsy and she was not.* Understand? . . . I was a Gypsy.
>
> You remember how good she was, even to the point of washing my feet— on the floor—on her knees, like a slave, when I was ill. (As you know, I bathe a lot and never have my feet dirty.) And that memory is always with me. [Pepe's mother died in 1964.] She was like a mother, and, when I was sick, the only mother at my side because my mother is my mother, but she had the *zambra* and had to be in charge when I could not go.

In spite of a sharp increase in Spanish tourism (upon which all of the *zambras* operating in the Sacro Monte are exceedingly dependent), the multiplicity of *zambra* enterprises today, competition from new nightclubs and hotels, and

"That olla *we like to make"*

payoffs to guides and tour leaders have combined to intensify rather than diminish the jealousy and feuding among Gypsies to which Isabel made earlier reference. Gypsy individualism is highly prized, even when it services exploitative situations, for example, price undercutting. Living with problems of poor health, the shortage of good flamenco performers, and the diminishing Gypsy population of the Sacro Monte, Isabel's primary concerns continue to center on her family and her *chicas* [the young *gitanas* in the *cuadros*].

"TO CARRY THEIR HOMES WELL"

I am able to lead, to sing, to have my business. . . . my Gypsy art with my *chicas*. What I desire is to be as I am, right now, always, and that my family have no bad sickness. *What a father does nobody else can do.* I don't ask for grand things, only the means of life. To be able to have food, and to present myself when I go into the street "as a person." . . . . To have little grief, and the *alegría*, Berta, the *alegría*! My ambience requires it—that to all the world I present a smile. Even if I were dead, there would be a smile on my lips!

Right now the thing I lack is the *turismo* [*zambra* clients] because that is my life and, naturally, one hopes it will go well. I worry for all my girls who work for me. I am responsible for them. They say, "Isabel, look how few tourists are coming!" and I reassure them and say, "Now that it is vacation time, tourists will come from all over the world, and you will earn money." . . . What I wish for in life is that all the *chicas*, my Gypsies, earn enough to carry their homes well.

And when they earn money, they are happy with their *patrona*. . . . That's what I desire, that tourism does not drop off in Granada. That many tourists

come—Americans, French, Germans, Italians—and that they visit my caves—
those very typical caves I have. So Gypsy! so full of copper! And that they shout,
";Olé! This is good art."

"That's the way we are, different from you"

And so, I do not want luck for myself alone. But for *all* my Gypsies because
they should be able to live a good life, without worry. . . . Already you know
the life of the Sacro Monte. . . . We live a life very different than yours.
. . . For example, the Gypsy will say, "Today I have earned 500 *pesetas*" . . .
and then it gives us joy to go down to Granada, wearing a *mantón*, with style!
And all the people of Granada look at us, well perfumed—a Spanish carnation
in the hair (after all, *I am La Golondrina*). . . . and even if I go in non-Gypsy
clothes, I always like to go with a carnation in my hair—a rose—or even only
a green leaf, so that people will say, "What an appealing Gypsy!"

This is the difference in our life. . . . *You* earn money and say "I'll save this
for that—and that for this." *We* earn a thousand *pesetas* and spend it. We do
not worry about tomorrow. . . . A lot of it we spend for food—because Gypsies
like food a great deal. That *olla* we like to make with its veal, sausages, cabbage,
and ground crusts of ham. Even though tomorrow we won't even have one
peseta . . . that day that we get the money, we enjoy ourselves. We spend it
all, and we have a feast.

One day runs into another. . . . We enjoy life in a different way than you do.
That's the way we are—different from you. That life satisfies us. . . . That is the
Gypsy way of life. THAT'S WHY WE ARE GYPSIES.

6

Children of the Sacro Monte

ONE OF THE MOST EFFECTIVE MEANS by which the Gypsies appear to insure cultural conservation is by permitting their children almost total participation in the adult world. Children may be seen not only performing in Gypsy *zambras*, engaged in selling various local commodities, and helping in other economic enterprises but fully participating in adult social affairs, family meetings, and, in short, in virtually all other adult activities as well.

A twelve-year-old Gypsy boy, Pepito, whose life progress we have followed over a decade, attends school until 4:00 P.M. daily, studies the guitar in the late afternoon, and then performs as a dancer/guitarist in the family *zambras* until all paying guests have left the Sacro Monte. In spite of the hours spent away from the caves while in school, Pepito is fully aware of family intragroup tensions and feuding, financial problems, and its shifting needs and wants. There is no one moment in the Gypsy child's life when he begins to participate in the decision-making process, but the child's early earning power and involvement in adult affairs prepares him for this role at a relatively young age.

For the most part, children seem to regulate their sleeping hours according to adult habits, and there appear to be few rituals to adults which children are expected to observe. In general, the Gypsy attitude toward children is extremely permissive, aggression seems to be encouraged, and most children, whether blood kin or not, tend to be treated with affection and kindness.

Among older children, beatings and other forms of physical punishment —pinching, even kicking—are utilized in the enculturative process, but these outbursts of violence directed at children are in most instances short-lived and followed by overt demonstrations of reconciliation. Because, as Mary Ellen Goodman has noted, "the child's level of expectation becomes adjusted to what is current among the people around him . . . what might be felt as deprivation or personal injury is likely to be accepted matter-of-factly when it is a commonplace of the child's society" (1967:110).

Exceptions, as, for example, in the case of Feli, which will be discussed in another section of this chapter, are rare, and unkind treatment of very young children is practically nonexistent.

The child also benefits in the extended kin situation prevalent among Gypsies in that his needs may be met by any number of adult relatives, many of whom influence his development. The boy whose parents send him off to school in the morning without food may find a devoted cousin waiting for him with bread and cheese at the school entrance; the girl left with younger siblings in her care will be helped by neighbors and relatives who pity her her young burdens. Indeed, Gypsies appear to compete often for the affections of children other than their own, and with great pride will point out the child who prefers their company to that of his own parents. Children learn quickly to capitalize on adult competition for their affections, opportunistically moving from cave to cave collecting food and adding to their material stores and creating an ever-shifting child population in terms of any one home.

Gypsy informants throughout Andalusia have advanced the unsolicited information to us that no Gypsy children are ever abandoned, "as are children of your people." To this, one added, "There are no Gypsy orphans. If the mother and father are dead, others care for the children as their own, and make no distinction between them."

A return visit to the Fajardo-Maya Gypsies in 1963, following that year's winter floods, introduced us to Carolina, a fourteen-year-old girl whose family had been drowned. So natural was this child's presence in an unrelated Gypsy family believed to be that no attempt at formal introduction nor explanation was made. She was now a member of a new family, engaging in precisely the same kind of activities as everyone else, and treated with no recognizable distinctions.

Although in a sense this fact was used by the Gypsies to point up the superior (in their thinking) quality of their own practices as compared to others, in the main it was offered as a flat statement of the only *natural* way for children to be treated. Inherent in it was a curiosity about people who felt the need to maintain orphanages, and who, if even but occasionally, practiced child abandonment. In a pertinent statement, Block noted that among the Gypsies "parents cling to their children as closely as the children cling to them. The Gypsy takes good care of what he values, and he values children highly" (1939:96).

The most notable exception to the observation regarding the kind treatment of children was among the so-called beggar Gypsies of the Sacro Monte, whom other Gypsies claimed were not Gypsies at all but, rather, individuals recruited from the lowest classes of Spanish society. Among the beggars it appeared that infants and very young children were used primarily to attract the sympathies of non-Gypsy populations and of tourists, much as described by Grellmann more than a century and a half ago.

> They go about in the guise of *beggars*—a character they well know how to support, and commonly carry with them a couple of children, miserably exposed to the cold and frost; one of these is lead by the hand, the other tied in a cloth to the woman's back, in order to excite compassion in well-disposed people. Whole troops of these Gypsy beggars are met with in Spain; and the encounter is by no means pleasant, as they ask alms in a manner, and with such importunity, as if they thought you could not deny them (1807:59).

On one occasion a young, ragged mother was seen viciously twisting the nose of her six-month-old infant in order, by the baby's crying, to add a realistic note to her claim that the baby was suffering from hunger. There appeared, also, to be good reason to believe that some of the babies carried in arms by the beggars were drugged in order to keep them asleep during the long hours of begging near hotels and at bus stops, but there was no way to verify this suspicion. Likewise, there was no way to check the validity of the beggars' claims to be Gypsies, a claim which non-Gypsies from Spain and other European countries were reported to have found useful in extorting money from tourists in recent years; nor was there any way to establish the truth of the Gypsies' violent assertions that the beggars were *not* real Gypsies. In any event, it was apparent that the beggars were a source of embarrassment to many of the Gypsies and that there is a decided trend toward disassociation from them and their means of livelihood.

"Just a Little Schooling"

As revealed in Chapter 4, the dependence of Andalusian Gypsies on oral tradition to inculcate and reinforce attitudes, behaviors, and beliefs in harmony with the thematic content of the culture was an important aspect of the enculturative process. Deep Song, while regarded as an integral part of that process, was not the only means employed for this purpose, nor was its importance considered to be as great today among Granada's performing Gypsies as it was in the past. Reasons given for its diminishing significance centered on the shortage of expert singers and the influence of tourism, formal education, and modern technology on the "teachings of the songs." With respect to outside interests, the greater independence and materialistic inclinations of the younger generation were cited as cause for some concern, while formal education and technology were related to the weakening of the influence of oral tradition as an enculturative vehicle. The fact is, however, that Gypsy children quite accurately reflect adult motivations, drives, and desires—their "materialism," for instance, being no more nor less than a carbon copy of its adult model. The "changes" identified by Gypsy informants as significant in the cultural patterning of children are in reality rather minor reworkings of traditional practices, which are viewed with a calculated regard for their immediate practicality rather than long-range consequences. The "what" of cultural transmission is less changed than the "how," and even the changing "how" tends to be traditionally framed.

Gypsy children of more affluent families, for example, are encouraged to attend school primarily in order to acquire fundamental literacy skills, which are viewed as essential to protect Gypsy interests in dealings with outsiders. Poorer children, especially the very young, may be permitted to attend school briefly for reasons which have little to do with learning. Parents of these children tend to view the school as a place where children are cared for while they work, and where—via free lunch programs—the family food budget is cut. Rarely are children permitted to attend school beyond age twelve, and frequent and prolonged absences operate to keep actual achievement at a very low level. This is not to say that Gypsies are devoid of pride in these accomplishments. On the contrary, they tend to infuse them with the same degree of ethnocentrism that is apparent in all aspects of Gypsy culture.

As Isabel expressed it,

Look, the *castellano* [Spaniard] is very different from us. Their culture is different—they have in their heads to become lawyers, architects, doctors—to do big things. As we do not have those ideas, we look at the *alegría*—the JOY—the dance, the arts. That is the truth. It is therefore much more *meritorio* (meritorious) that *we* know how to read and write. Understand? Because most of us go to school at the same time that we have to earn in order to eat. Many dance and don't go to school at all. But those who have a little dignity and want to advance, go to school in the mornings and dance in the *zambra* at night or into the morning. . . . And therefore under those circumstances, they learn to read and write a little, and then that is more to their credit. *You* are born to learn that, while we must work, and so for us, even to learn to sign our names is a great thing. *And that is worth more in us than in you.*

The distinctions made between Spaniards and Gypsies and, indeed, our-selves, regarding occupational and educational goals reinforce this same inform-ant's account of Gypsy origins.

El Señor [the Lord] when he went to Heaven, first called an assembly of all the peoples of the world in the Great Plaza. (This is a tale of mine.) He said, "Tomorrow I am going to Heaven, and those who want to come here before I go, to them I will assign their position in life. Whoever gets there too late, won't get any—no? (¡*Claro!*)" And that way before he left, he assigned every-one a position—a school teacher, a doctor, all. And there were two Gypsies who were very lazy, and one said to the other, "Look, Cousin, the Lord is leaving today. He is going to Heaven, and everyone has already gone to get their destinies. We are going to be late." And so they started running to the Plaza, and when they got there, the Lord was already leaving because they were so lazy. By the time they ran to the Great Plaza, he was leaving and they called to Him, "But, Father, you have assigned to everyone in the world a destiny. Are you just going to go off and leave the Gypsies here without an assigned place?" . . . . The Lord said, "You get on any way you can." . . . And so he left us, and so we get on any way we can. We eat, but wait. This legend is mine, but it is a reality. The Gypsies live or eat by their wits. They have no real assigned place in the world.

In spite of the seeming acceptance of their *hado*—"to eat, but wait"—Isabel, her husband, daughter, nephew, and eventually her grandchildren, have all attended school, have prospered through various family enterprises, and regard the founding of the Ave-María School in the Sacro Monte as one of the most important events in the history of Granada.

We went to that very good school—the Ave-María School—founded in the Sacro Monte by Father Manjón, a priest who was very, very good. . . . A Father who gave alms for his Gypsies. As he would walk along the paths, and see a Gypsy barefooted, he would say, "Tomorrow, come to the school," and when he would see a pregnant Gypsy, he would say, "Come to the school," and he would give her *el hatico* [layette for the baby] and food. He would give the Gypsies food in the school. . . . That man was a God to all.

He started the school in a cave, there in the cave he taught the Gypsies, and he would go through the streets of Granada asking the people for alms to help support it. Brick by brick, he built it, all for his Gypsies of the Sacro Monte. . . . All that he wanted was for his Gypsies to know how to read and write, and he died with the joy of knowing that he had taught them. He is a saint.

You can see the school—it is all there—even the original cave. It is on the Camino del Sacro Monte, and also the new buildings. . . . Even the new school is for his Gypsies.

Las Escuelas del Ave-María

Opened in 1889, the Ave-María School now consists of thirteen buildings and a chapel. It is situated in more than two-thirds of a mile of gardens above the Darro River, in a location of incredible beauty. Part of the Sacro Monte, and sharing with its Gypsy neighbors the view of the Alhambra which faces it, the school is within easy walking distance of the *cuevas*. In a biography of its founder, Don Andrés Manjón y Manjón, he is described on its opening day, eighty years ago, as surrounded by *"gitanillos medio desnudos"* (half-naked Gypsy childen) in the small Gypsy cave in which the first class of the famous school was conducted (1946:114).

In 1968 there were more than seven hundred students enrolled in its eight primary grades. Its director, Manuel Pino Sabio, like Father Manjón, appeared dedicated to the cause of the Gypsies, although the school's student population was overwhelmingly non-Gypsy. Of the three hundred and seventy boys, only thirty were Gypsy; while even fewer Gypsy girls enrolled.

Invited to visit the school by Gypsy children with whom we had worked, we were enthusiastically met by them at the school's gates on the appointed first day. A holiday atmosphere prevailed—due in part to the children's own pride and pleasure in "their" school and, in no small measure, to the fact that the presence of their "American friends" served to free them from classes for a few hours at least. We were introduced to Señor Pino and the school's headmistress and permitted to visit classes, talk with children, and observe varied activities. From its very inception, the school's pedagogical orientation has been characterized by a high degree of progressivism, unusual in Spanish parochial curricula. Predating the famed Montessori method, the school's use of games, mosaics, and other advanced teaching devices has been held to account for its success in working with Gypsy children. In addition, the devotion of Father Manjón to "his Gypsies," virtually transformed into legend by succeeding generations of *gitanos*, continues to permeate the school's atmosphere. Feeling welcomed and secure within the school's confines, Gypsy children were reported by Señor Pino to function effectively in its program, albeit home-related behavioral problems, absenteeism, and such were viewed as deterrents to achievement.

The director of the school proved to be one of our greatest sources of information concerning the problems of Gypsy children, educational and otherwise. He gave freely of his time, as did the headmistress, and seemed wholly dedicated to understanding and furthering the development of this younger generation. While the majority of Gypsy children who attend his school appeared to be well fed and clothed, and difficult to distinguish from non-Gypsies, some are from exceedingly impoverished families. Parents of these children must be persuaded by the school priest to permit the children to attend. Such parents were reported to be so uncommunicative and indifferent that the school even had to assign approximate birthdates to the children for use in the school's records. In addition, the school assumed the responsibility of teaching even the most basic norms of behavior, for example, eating habits. The small fees for feeding these children are personally assumed by the director, directress, or the priest.

Regardless of age, all Gypsy children entering the school are assigned to the first grade, with boys and girls separated. Frequent play periods and other outdoor activities appear to negate some of the expected self-consciousness that this practice generates, older children being provided with opportunities for contact with students in more advanced grades.

In spite of their obvious pride in their school, poorer Gypsy boys are apparently sensitive about their Gypsy status. When reported for fighting with non-Gypsy children (a rather frequent occurence), they express the feeling that they are being discriminated against because they are Gypsies. While they are occasionally taunted by non-Gypsy children from the Albaicín, most of the taunts are actually nonprejudicial in nature. Encouraged from birth by their mothers to display their *hombría* (manliness), physical aggression in Gypsy boys tends to be an acting out of masculine behavior for which they are rewarded in their own culture. The marked emphasis on masculinity also is reflected in early maternal pride in the baby's penis and pseudosexual behavior, which gives way by school age to overt sex gestures, presenting, and so forth, in prepubescent boy–girl relationships. These, as has been noted previously, do not culminate, even in later years, in actual sexual intercourse, the virginity of Gypsy girls being held sacred, but do serve to provide boys with the sense of reinforcing their manliness. Contrary to findings in studies of other cultures, "momism" among Gypsies does not produce homosexuality but rather appears to insure its virtual nonexistence among them. The male child is aggrandized and praised for manlike actions only. He is not expected ever to help with chores associated with the female role, nor to assume a subservient position in male–female relationships.

Gypsy children who perform in the *zambras*, like adult dancers, create the illusion of intense sexuality, a fact which tourists often misinterpret as the sanctioning of sexual promiscuity. This form of behavior, as well as fighting, is often emulated through school contacts by non-Gypsy boys, as are certain forms of begging "for the sport of it."

Behavioral problems among the twenty Gypsy girls enrolled in the Ave-María School tend to be very minor and relate primarily to absenteeism among the very poor children. In the main, these children appear to be shy, somewhat withdrawn, and sensitive about the poor quality of their clothing. They shared, nevertheless, with more affluent Gypsies and non-Gypsy students, pride in even the most minor of scholastic accomplishments, signing their own names, and the like, and almost appeared to bask visibly in the kindness of their teachers. In their home lives many of these children have to fend largely for themselves. School, for them, represents a brief interlude between a gentle, protective milieu and the harsh realities of the Gypsy world. In general, the motivation to learn stems largely from the school atmosphere and from self-motivation rather than from parental encouragement or pressure. Children tend to regard even the briefest exposure to the Ave-María School as the equivalent of a Harvard degree, albeit, their aspirations and loyalties appear to remain Gypsy centered.

"I Wish . . . , I Wish"

Anxious to identify the nature of the hopes, aspirations and fears of a representative group of Gypsy school children, we selected ten children, all of whom were in middle childhood. Having had more than two years of experience in attending school, verbally precocious, old enough to have crystallized their wishes concerning the future, the children were asked to consider a series of six questions, five of which were suggested by Cantril's Self-Anchoring Striving Scale (1965:22–23):

1. What in your life makes you happiest now?
2. What makes you saddest now?
3. What do you think would make you happiest when you grow up?
4. What do you like best about Gypsy life?
5. What would you change in order that Gypsies might be happier?

The sixth was phrased as follows:

6. If you could have three wishes come true, what would you wish for? Think about this carefully, and tell us tomorrow; decide which wish is most important, and which is least important.

A young English interpreter who had established close and prolonged ties with these children insured that the questions were fully understood by them.

Nine of the children returned the following day anxious to have their

"I wish . . . , I wish" (Author Lois Floyd, right)

thoughts recorded and exhibiting extremely serious attitudes toward the project. This attitude, contrary to casual expectation, was sustained throughout subsequent interview sessions with them. Indeed, it was necessary to intercede in the several squabbles which centered on whose "turn" it was next, who would go "first," and so on. In addition, the children tended to be highly secretive with one another about their responses, and were pleased with the privacy accorded their individual sessions with us, conducted in an enclosed cave patio. All signed their names with exaggerated flourishes in our notebooks and, with great displays of self-importance, flaunted their select status in front of younger Gypsy children. Parents of the tenth child were suspicious of our intent and refused to permit him to return.

As with their adult counterparts, Gypsy child informants were closely associated with *zambra* activities and affected by the influences of Sacro Monte cave life. While the majority of these children were well cared for at home, their responses to our questions revealed a rather wide range of child-care antecedents and stress areas which were varied in both nature and intensity. Conversely, homogeneity in terms of wishes, goals, and fears was also noted, substantiating in part Cantril's observations concerning basic uniformities in human aspirations. The role of Gypsy culture in shaping the specifics of their aspirations, however, was found to be more revealing in the responses of the children than even in those of adults similarly questioned. The three profiles which follow communicate the diversity as well as the similarity of cultural experience and expectation in middle childhood.

PEPITO, AGE 12. "I am happiest when I am playing the guitar because it is easier than dancing. You don't sweat."

Pepito was raised by his aunt and uncle for ten years and calls them "Mama" and "Papa." His biological parents are professional flamenco performers who are frequently "on tour" in the United States and other countries and cities away from Granada. As noted earlier, this child attends school, takes professional guitar lessons, and performs from 5 o'clock in the afternoon until 1 A.M. nightly in the *zambra*. An excellent guitarist, he alternates between dancing and playing in the family *cuadros*. In the absence of more mature performers, he assumes the adult male role in the traditional dances. In the role of "bridegroom," for example, he manages to convince audiences of his *hombría*. Fair-haired and handsome, Pepito and his friend Dolores are applauded for their adultlike precocity and appear to enjoy participation in *zambra* activities. In spite of long hours at work and practice, he cites "the art and the joy of life" as best in Gypsy culture, and stated that he would change it only by requiring all Gypsies to learn to dance "as a group."

DOLORES, AGE 12. The most mature of our child informants, Dolores is Pepito's constant companion, and they refer to one another as *novios*. The nature of this girl's home life is suggested by her wishes and responses to several of our questions. "I wish most that my family would get along well together, and give to others what they need, while others give to my family what we need." In contemplating the future, the saddest projection for this child was the possibility of being married to a man who beat her. She would like to see "fighting among Gypsies stopped," while the best of Gypsy life was expressed as, "When Gypsies get together, make parties, dance, and don't fight." Dolores was the only member of her family performing in *zambras*, a job she had held for four years. Torn between two worlds, she is happiest now "when I come home from school to study and see the books," but her future wish for herself is "to go abroad as a Gypsy dancer."

FELI, AGE 10. "The money—the money."

Unlike Pepito and Dolores, Feli is from a very poor Gypsy family. Her name, ironically, means "joy." Her parents are ragpickers who live in one of the primitive Sacro Monte caves without electricity, water, or any other conveniences. She has three younger brothers, and is responsible for the care also of a twelve-month-old sister, all five children sharing a communal bed. Adult informants reported that these children "live like animals" and receive virtually no care in the home—for example, they never "sit down to a meal." For Feli, both present and future were summed up in one blunt word, "money." She is mistreated by her father and beaten by him frequently. This fact caused her grave embarrassment, and only after establishing very close rapport with one of us was she able to verbalize this sadness. Starved for affection, this little girl would endeavor to establish as close physical contact with "Luisa" as possible, her usual facial expression of profound sorrow giving way under kind response to one of quiet worship. One of the children who erratically attends the Ave-María School, Feli's food is paid for there by the directress of the girl's division. Gypsy neighbors, "those who live beside me," were identified by Feli as the best part of Gypsy life. (Neighbors were known to help her with the baby, to save food scraps for her, and, in one instance, to let her watch their television set when her father was away.) In spite of the gross deprivation which characterizes Feli's life and the atypical rejection of her father, her first wish was to live a long time "with the Gypsies." She seemed devoted to her mother, whom she described as "beautiful." Knowing that we would be at a *zambra* one night, Feli was found waiting at the doorway with her mother—a shy, adult copy of Feli, pathetically clad, bruised and work worn, and looking decades older than her approximate thirty years. Wanting to be like the "Virgin Mary" when she grows up, Feli's more immediate wish was that "they don't cut off the water" to the public well on which she has to depend.

Among our remaining child informants, boys ranging from ten to twelve years old, we observed all of the usual personality variables that even the most narrow of cultural backgrounds seem unable to homogenize. Mario, age 12, typified in his swagger and confidence the idealized dominance of the Gypsy male. Contrasting with the quicksilverish behavior of José (Pepito's lieutenant), the youngest of our informants, Manuel, was thoughtful, quiet, agonizing over even the simplest of questions. In spite of the secretiveness with which the children guarded their answers, some rather remarkable similarities emerged from our analysis of the data with which they provided us. The major concerns of these children centered on violence in Gypsy culture and/or family life, death, and the nature of interpersonal relationships with non-Gypsies—"Spaniards." In responding to the query "What makes you saddest now?" typical answers included the following:

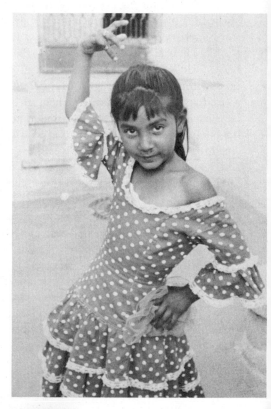

Gypsy Children
of the Sacro Monte

When I fight with friends. (Manolo)
When someone dies. (Pepito)
If a brother or someone dies in my family. (Melchor)
When Gypsies and Spaniards fight and die. (Dolores)
When my father beats me. (Feli)
When my parents fight with other people, and my friends say insults to me. (Antonio)

In identifying changes they would like to see in Gypsy life, informants tended to emphasize similar themes. "If I could change Gypsy life, there would be no Gypsy fights. I would separate them and explain that fighting is foolish." Melchor's concept of desirable change was echoed by Dolores and by the aggressive Mario, who somewhat surprisingly stated, "I would like Gypsies and Spaniards to get along together better. If I were the government, I would pass a law saying that they could not fight nor carry knives. Then no one would be hurt."

Other hopes for the Gypsy future included education, money, and, in one case, "to make it possible for everyone to have a flat." Often, education and money were combined, as, for example,

I would like for all Gypsies to go to school, and for each to have two million pesetas. (Manolo)
I would give them alms and help teach them to do things when they are older. (José)
I would change Gypsy life by sending them to school and giving them money. (Antonio)

While these responses quite obviously reflected their special status—that is, Gypsy school children—they also tended to reinforce the adult view of education as a means primarily of improving finances within the traditional Gypsy framework rather than by "doing big things." Feli's conclusion, "I would make all Gypsies as good as the Spaniards," was followed by the wish to "always live with Gypsies."

Answers to questions concerning happiness now and when grown up tended to show somewhat greater variability and reflected, too, some of the usual responses of children everywhere to such queries: "To play football." "To go to the beach with my teacher." "To go to the movies with my friends." "To win the football pool." The last response is, in fact, the almost universal wish of all poor people in Spain, who associate the dream of a better life with the Spanish lottery system. The Gypsy children who singled out this possibility for future happiness linked it to buying better homes for their families, cars, and other material necessities. In all ranked orders of preference, family welfare was placed first, with the child's own wishes, for example, to have a set of toy electric cars, subordinated to parental needs. Four of the children added "having a flat down in the town" to their ideas of future happiness and wish expressions. Other areas to which present happiness was related included:

That my friends play with me and that they don't fall out with me. (Manolo)
When one of my family marries and we have a wedding fiesta. (Melchor)

Future happiness was expressed as:

To get a *novia* and then to marry. (Pepito)
To have a home with my wife. (Melchor)
For my parents to see me married by the Church. (José)
To look for a *novia*. (Antonio)
To know a lot. (Manuel)

The importance accorded marriage by these children was most seriously expressed by them to us and was completely devoid of traces of preadolescent self-consciousness or precocity. They meant what they said, *"It is the Gypsy way."*

The responses of the children concerning their areas of unhappiness and desired change in Gypsy life may create the impression of a culture dominated by violence and tragedy. Actually, this is a distortion of the Gypsy ethos. When asked what they liked *best* about Gypsy life, these same children answered:

The Art. . . . the *alegría* of the life. (Pepito)
Gypsies can sing and dance from childhood. (Mario)
When the Gypsies get together and make parties and dance. (Dolores)
The flamenco. (Manolo)
The whole group [Gypsies] and the *zambra*. (Melchor)
The *zambra*. (Antonio)

Feli, whose life experiences were negative in the extreme, looked to "those who live beside me" as representative of the best in Gypsy culture. Exposed as a peripheral onlooker to the constant preparations made by these Gypsies in their commercial *zambra* enterprises, she, too, associated "the arts" with the best in her life, that is, good and small kindnesses. Her wish, "to live a long time, and with Gypsies," was coupled with the hope that she would be "treated well." Asked if she would like to marry, she responded, "How should I know?", a not surprising answer, given her home conditions.

The idea of fiestas and Gypsy "joy" was found linked, sometimes in curious juxtaposition, to many of the wishes expressed by the children. For example, Dolores wished for her sister's first communion in the Catholic Church so that it could be followed by a one-day fiesta. She projected a *two-day* fiesta for her own wedding "in white," demonstrating, we guess, the universality of the rising costs of marriage. Through the influence of the school, its director pointed out that more Spanish customs, many of which are religious in nature, are being adopted by Gypsy children and their families. The wish "to be married in white" (that is, to have a church wedding) was expressed not only by the girls in our sample but by the boys as well (Pepito, Mario, and others). Such weddings are regarded as indicative of high status, but invariably are followed by traditional Gypsy ceremonies and celebrations.

Boys' wishes, beyond those relating to the acquisition of material possessions ("a car like Pepe's," for example), focused on marriage, family, health, and occupational goals.

I want to have a home with children. (Melchor)
To look for a house and find it. (Antonio)
That all of my family could have good health and never be sick. (Pepito)
To be a footballer. (Manolo, Antonio, and Mario)
To be a mechanic. (Manuel and José)

Occupational goals were never given primary preference but rather were viewed as the means through which family-centered wishes could be realized. "To be a footballer"—that is, to play soccer professionally—has replaced, as it has in Spain in general, the former ambition to be a bullfighter. It will be recalled that Gypsies have excelled in the bullfight, albeit none of our informants displayed interest in this aspect of flamenco life. Mechanical ambitions tended to reflect both the boys' preoccupation with cars, of which only a few are owned by the sedentary Gypsies of Granada, and the traditional acceptance of metalworking as a suitable "male" occupation. Some Gypsies do outstanding body repair work on automobiles, often using the hand metalworking techniques that have been passed down through generations of Gypsy men.

Pepito and Dolores did not consider occupational goals in the manner usual to children, that is, "when I grow up." Regular members of a *zambra* group since early childhood, they were already doing what they will be doing in adult years. Pepito's guitar study was viewed with greater seriousness than his dancing, while Dolores saw change only in the possibility of "going abroad" as a dancer.

Señor Pino noted that some Gypsy parents today discourage this form of livelihood for their children, while others pay for some professional training in order to insure that they will become sufficiently proficient in the flamenco arts to earn professional contracts *away* from the caves. One consequence of this change, he stated, is that "[t]he *zambras* of the Sacro Monte are less authentic today than ten years ago." Because the better artists perform in nightclubs, hotels, and/or "on tour," the Gypsies engaged in performing in the caves, with some notable exceptions, tend to be less gifted performers—often those who have passed their prime or who, like Pepito and Dolores, are children in the process of learning.

"If I Were the Government . . ."

The wishes and preoccupations of the nine children we have discussed were, in the main, reinforcements of the traditional themes we identified in Chapter 3, that is, Gypsy pride, preoccupation with death or fate, loyalty, and freedom. Educational and occupational goals still emphasize the need for income without loss of freedom and are group oriented. However, Ocaña's observation that "when they can sign their names and *engañar a los payos* [exploit non-Gypsies] that is enough!" (1963:47) did not appear to be substantiated by our data. Children wished for better Gypsy/non-Gypsy relationships, exhibited strong feeling about intercultural conflicts, and regarded some aspects of Spanish life— "to be married in white," "to have a flat down in the town," "to have a little education"—as very desirable. Mario's "If I were the government, I would pass a law saying . . ." reflected the trend we noted previously of greater Gypsy dependency on local law.

At the same time, these children adhered closely to Gypsy traditions, expressing such wishes as "to find a *novia*" (a Gypsy wife) and "to live always with Gypsies." School and church teachings appeared to influence little the Gypsy tendency to live for the moment, with all of the children emphasizing the *alegría* of Gypsy life, its fiestas and *zambras*, as its most outstanding quality. Standing in sharp contrast to its violent aspects, which were both feared and accepted as a *natural* part of their reality world, its moments of *alegría* operated to reinforce their loyalties and pride in group membership to an extreme degree.

Children, like adults, placed contradictory concepts in juxtaposition—"I would like God to give me a little *luck* so that I could earn money to look after my wife and children." They also demonstrated a curious mixture of mature social consciousness and childlike naïveté in their hopes and fears. Dolores' wish that her family "give to others what they need, while others give to my family what we need," was followed by the observation that she was saddest "when I fall down and hurt myself and cry." The wish for a toy car and the desire for improved family welfare were assigned varying priorities, but, nevertheless, incorporated the hopes of these children for the good life—their *Gypsy* life.

"The Babies Come Out Dancing"

While more Gypsy children are being encouraged, or, in poorer families, permitted to attend school (Ocaña's twenty-five Sacro Monte Gypsy school children having been doubled in a five-year period), the majority of Gypsy children continue to learn in a largely school-free environment. Imitation, nonrestrictive cultural participation, and encouragement to emulate adult activities and occupations at a very early age still constitute the norm in the enculturative process. The widely held belief in innate ability, and traditional attitudes regarding the superiority of informal versus formal teaching, tend to negate or significantly modify school influences. As noted by Isabel,

> Look—here we do not have any academies, no one to teach us the song or the dance. The only thing is that when we are pregnant, from the first day [of conception] we continue to work.
>
> Now the little Gypsy is fat—she dances—one day after another—until the nine months are up. She stops dancing in the *zambra*—she goes to her *cueva*— and then, at the right moment she gives birth. *That way, with Gypsies, the babies come out dancing.*
>
> When they are only one or two months old, we lift them in our hands, up and down, and we work their hands, and snap our fingers, . . . By the time they are a year and one-half, they start to put one foot in front of the other . . . to *zapatear* [to beat time with their feet], and by the time they are grown, the ones who are *born* for that, they know how. They are filled with the art. Once in a while, one is a great born artist—a real professional—who goes to America, or Madrid, or who has contracts in many places. . . . But, this is a born artist from birth. No academies, nor does anyone teach them [professionally].

Isabel, curiously, does not regard herself as a teacher, although she has instructed a generation of dancers and singers. Her methods, while "natural" to her, would be regarded as quite professional by almost any standards other than her own. Nevertheless, the sight of babies being placed on tables and encouraged to move their hands and feet to the accompaniment of adult *pitos* and hand clapping is a common one, as is the inevitable display of approval and affection greeting even the slightest suggestion of infant "talent."

Actually, some professional training, frequently via assignment to a dance master or known guitarist, is part of the experience of the more accomplished Gypsy artists. However, in the Sacro Monte, virtually all children informally learn aspects of the flamenco arts. While not all are encouraged to develop them, a few are ruthlessly exploited by parents who view them as marketable flamenco commodities. Cruelly treated, the training of these children is characterized by brutal beatings and tense hours of practice and performance. They rarely attend school and clandestinely move about the Sacro Monte in search of brief moments of rest.

Our emphasis on the learning of the flamenco arts, an emphasis which derives from the particular group of Gypsies with whom we have worked most consistently, should not be misinterpreted, however, as the only kind of occupational learning taking place among Granada's Gypsies. In fact, only a minority follow this form of livelihood in adult years. The range of life choices, while undergoing some expansion in recent years, continues to be narrow for most children, and defined in tradtional terms. Accordingly, their enculturation is less characterized by diversity than is the case in a society such as our own. Diversity does exist, however, perhaps more among Gypsies with their traditional honoring of individualism than in other contemporary folk or peasant cultures. The term ¡Qué gitano! continues to communicate the idea of individual style, wit, and gracia, and Gypsy children learn early to perform in the culture in ways that meet adult approval. The homogeneity of adult expectation and concomitant child-rearing practices insures among Gypsy children that they acquire knowledge,

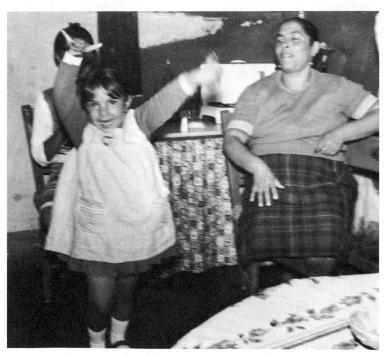

"The babies come out dancing"

attitudes, and behaviors appropriate to their culture, on the one hand, and that they learn, on the other, to transcend that homogeneity in permissible individualized ways.

The poor children of La Chana may appear to fend largely for themselves, but they have been taught, in both explicit and implicit ways, to cope with this need. By the time they are left to their own devices by working parents, these children display remarkable adaptation to the terms by which their lives must be lived and managed. Life's moments of violence, hunger, and tragedy, which for many of these children are more frequent than those of Gypsy *alegría*, represent culturally approved and shared norms. The child accepts the terms of his existence, and his "level of expectation becomes adjusted to what is current among the people around him" (Goodman 1967:110). This is not to say, however, that the levels do not change, nor that they should be prevented from changing. The recent establishment of a church-related "nursery" in the *barrio* appears to be transforming aspects of early childhood experience, which will be identified and discussed in a later chapter. In the final analysis, the children of La Chana, like those of the Ave-María School in the Sacro Monte, will be the humble agents of selective change in a culture which has endured and thrived for more than five centuries in Alhambra shadows. But change is not new to Gypsies, and the phrase ¡*Qué gitano*! reflects as much the tolerance of change in Gypsy culture as it does the endurance of its uniqueness. Its children are the inheritors of that tradition, and they know it well.

7

Patrins of Change

Do not scorn me 'cause I'm poor.
You ne'er can tell! You ne'er can tell!
The world keeps turning like a wheel. . . .
And yesterday a tower fell!
                              Brown 1922:265

COMPARED TO OTHER PERIODS in history, the Gypsy today occupies a relatively secure position in Andalusian society. Tangible manifestations of this security are seen in present-day Andalusia in the growing numbers of Gypsy business enterprises. In writing of Gypsy industries in Granada (home of approximately 7 percent of Spain's estimated 50,000 Gypsies), Villajos calls attention to the fact that while the Gypsies continue to ply their traditional metalworking arts, their forges today are producing numerous articles which cater to Andalusian rather than to Gypsy taste (1949:29). Aside from expanding their metalworking arts, it has been noted further that the Gypsies are currently entering the construction, carpentry, mechanical, and dressmaking trades. In addition, Gypsy women are found today in domestic service and working in the small home factories which produce handmade laces and embroidered goods. There are reports also of the slow movement of some few Gypsies into the professions, although no official estimates are available to date of their total number.

Observers of signs of greater security among Andalusian Gypsy populations are struck, too, by the modern improvements to be seen in their homes. Most of the remaining *cuevas* of Granada's Sacro Monte Gypsies are no longer "primitive" in the old sense of the word. Modern electrical equipment, telephones, substantial furnishings, television sets, a deep concern with outward appearances, and the gradual introduction of indoor plumbing have all combined to produce a sense of modern comfort in the Gypsies. A 1971 addition included a postage-stamp size swimming pool in one cave patio, so small that it overflowed when its proud owner demonstrated it to us! Even in the La Chana *barrio*, television antennas protrude like great exclamation marks from the rooftops of the poor homes beneath them.

There is need to spend but little time in southern Spain to recognize also the sense of practical indebtedness felt in certain Andalusian cities for the tourist-attracting "value" of their Gypsy populations. The concern of hotel proprietors and, indeed, the Spanish government, that the Gypsy arts be kept as free of corruption

Gypsy Life Styles

Sacro Monte

La Chana

as possible is advanced as strong evidence of the increasing value placed on pre-
serving the uniqueness and integrity of the previously outlawed Gypsy style.

To these materialistic *patrins* (signs) of greater Gypsy security and
permanence, observers today are inclined to add the less tangible symbol of a
more durable type of empathy which appears to have developed between Andalusian and Gypsy populations in recent years. Whether, as was advanced recently
by both Gypsy and Andalusian informants in Spain, this new empathy has its
roots in the shared horrors and hardships of the Spanish Civil War, or, as was
theorized also, it is the gradual and natural outgrowth of more than five centuries
of coexistence, the fact remains that acculturation has been greatly accelerated in
the last two decades. Although still loyal to basic Gypsy traditions and laws, the
Andalusian Gypsy today recognizes and, in general, supports local law as well.
As noted, among the sedentary populations, Gypsy children increasingly are being
encouraged by their parents to attend school at least to the point of acquiring
basic literacy skills. Spanning the period from 1959 to 1970, work with Andalusian
Gypsies has revealed a very minor trend toward a more "open" Gypsy attitude
concerning intermarriage between Gypsy and non-Gypsy, albeit these unions continue to be strongly discouraged. Among the sedentary Gypsies especially, a pronounced trend toward a more complete acceptance of Spanish Catholicism has
been noted, coincident with a more humane and sympathetic attitude adopted by
the church toward the Gypsy. The more significant of these changes are discussed
in the sections that follow, together with data relevant to current Gypsy hopes,
aspirations, and fears. Nonchanging aspects of their culture are manifest in the
Gypsy view of American culture, observations first recorded in 1964, and to which
we have subsequently added in following studies in Spain.

"You Will Eat, But You Will Not Work"

The traditional attitudes of Granada's Gypsies toward work were emphasized in the life history of Pepe, the *payo* whose marriage to a Gypsy woman
thirty years ago was discussed by her in Chapter 5. His daughter says of him,
"My father talks like a Gypsy, and feels like a Gypsy. He has lived among us for
many years, more than among his own people. He considers himself a Gypsy,
and the same is true of me."

Intimately involved in the life of the Sacro Monte and accepted by the
Gypsies of La Chana, Pepe's concerns and hopes centered principally on changing aspects of Gypsy culture. His association with the culture, however, was clearly
reflected in his recourse to its traditions and themes in discussing contemporary
problems. The Gypsy legend of Christ's blessing, for example, was utilized by
him to distinguish between the work attitudes of older and younger *gitanos*,
albeit his emphasis was focused primarily on Gypsy/non-Gypsy distinctions.

Look here, when they crucified Christ, he went carrying the cross to Calvary.
He asked for water, and no one would give Him water. Upon arriving at the
top of Calvary, some Gypsies gathered. They got water, and upon approaching
their Christ, they threw themselves at Him and gave Him water. He rested a

little and revived. He said, "You, the Gypsies, have my blessing. *You will eat, but you will not work.* And those who follow also will eat, but not work." That was Christ's blessing to the Gypsies. And I am one of them.

In interpreting this legend, Pepe, as well as other Andalusian informants, stressed in somewhat contradictory terms, the Gypsy's desire to improve his basic home conditions but his reluctance to view his life as work centered.

We work in order to live, for food, and for a little house. But, just to hoard *pesetas*, that, no. Stuck to the Gypsies, I earned 2 *pesetas*. That way I was able to become a person. But, *we do not throw away the light of life.*

In actuality, the majority of Sacro Monte Gypsies work throughout their lives engaged in relatively low-paying occupations and trades which require the expenditure of long hours and personal energy. Said one of these Gypsies,

We are enslaved here [by work in the *zambra*]. With this business, if we were not here the tour agencies would take the people to other caves and we would lose our clients. It is, therefore, an obligation to be here always. But over there [meaning the United States] work is regarded differently. Here, someone may say, "My mother is working, my father is working, therefore it is not necessary for me to work." That life in America is very rapid—very rapid. Whereas here everyone lives with *alegría* and more peace.

The effect of increased contact with non-Gypsies, especially via tourism, was viewed by the director of the Ave-María School as especially relevant to the growth of materialism among Gypsies and to their gradual movement into non-traditional occupations. Similarly, these contacts were viewed as influencing educational motivations and as the shaping force behind changing aspirations. In fact, however, the kind of work pursued by most Gypsy men differs little today from that of their grandfathers before them.

The emphasis in this informant's description of male occupations—that is, those who *really* work—points to the perpetuation of the rather limited range of jobs still considered appropriate for Gypsy men.

Gypsy men—those who really work—work in the forges. They work with iron, make things of copper, metalwork in general. That is what they *truly* work at. Others dedicate themselves to work as middlemen in the selling of horses, mules, donkeys. For example, you have a horse which you want to sell and I want to buy. Then we get the Gypsy to negotiate the sale, and we pay him for his services. Others apply themselves to the selling of materials which they buy here in the market—and then they go outside of Granada to the *pueblos* selling them. That is another form of work. And others are dedicated to the *zambra*—some sing, some dance, others play the guitar.

Despite the seeming contradictions of the data, the Gypsy attitude toward work remains traditionally and emotionally anchored. "Naturally, anywhere in the world, in order to eat you have to work." Accepting the need to work, the Gypsy weaves that need into the fabric of his life style. But he does not view work as an end in itself, nor does he invest his occupational pursuits, except where they happen to coincide with his pleasurable ones, with any significant degree of importance. With few exceptions, notably among outstanding *zambra* artists, he works because he must, and rarely with anything more than quite specific, immediate goals as his driving force.

"After That Meeting with the Pope . . ."

Among younger Gypsies, the acceptance of education and employment in trades, which bring them into closer contact with non-Gypsies, was attributed in part by informants to the effects of the audience granted to more than 3000 Gypsies by Pope Paul VI in 1965. Attracting Gypsies from countries such as Spain, France, Italy, England, the United States, the congress marked the first time in more than five centuries that a pope had encouraged a Gypsy pilgrimage to Rome, and the first time ever that a pope had celebrated mass in a Gypsy encampment. In describing Gypsy faith, Pope Paul noted that "exemplary faith, absolute obedience, and confidence in God, these are the virtues found at an elevated level in Gypsies" (*Newark News*: February 27, 1964).

Speaking of Nazi persecution, in which more than 400,000 Gypsies lost their lives as members of an "impure" race, Pope Paul observed a change in attitude today toward world "Gypsydom." "Here, he said, "you have a new experience: you find people who care for you, hold you in esteem." Extensive coverage by all forms of news media drew world attention to the historic congress, a fact cited by Gypsies as significant for them.

> Because the pope has decreed that no longer should there be distinctions made between Gypsies and *castellanos*—all should be "one," today Gypsies are becoming more modern. More are being educated from childhood by the school, and some are even entering professions and all that. These things are attracting the young—the old people, no. There are older people into whose heads this idea of progress does not enter. They are the really old ones. They want to go on living their same life. But it is with the young ones, now ten, and twenty years from now when they have become men, this is when they will notice the change in life. Right now, three years after that meeting with the pope, it is now that they take in the changes. This has gotten into their heads, and they are seeing a change in life—*plenty good.*

"While the Mothers Look for Life . . ."

The humanization of the Catholic Church's attitude toward Granada's Gypsies actually has been ongoing there for more than eighty years. It has produced a gradual Gypsy response, a response reported to have been accelerated in recent years by help provided impoverished Gypsies driven from their Sacro Monte cave homes in 1963, by the work of the Church in La Chana, by the influence of younger, more progressive Spanish priests, and by the effect of papal support of the Gypsy cause. The founding of the Department of Social Services for Gypsies, with its national headquarters in Madrid, also has drawn the attention of Spaniards to Gypsy problems; and its appeals reportedly have attracted volunteer support, both financial and in the form of contributed time, of educational, medical, and housing programs.

Our work in the *barrio* focused principally on the effects of these programs on Gypsy children, and parental attitudes regarding them. In discussing La Chana prior to our first visit there (a visit facilitated by the fact that many of its Gypsy residents were former Sacro Monte cave dwellers with whom we had worked in previous years and with whom we had continued contact via their participation in *zambra* activities), Pepe noted:

> Those who live down in that new *barrio* used to live in this one. Here there were very big inundations [flooding in the caves] and they became frightened of the caves because some people drowned. . . . And because of these changes and other innovations made by the Church, . . . the Church is very much involved in helping them. . . . All of these things are giving them much animation. The church workers are prepared to do all this because while I could take those children, I am not qualified to educate them. I could give them as much as I have, but I do not have within me the resources to give them more than that. Now these men and women who dedicate themselves exclusively to those things are giving them the education they need. Without knowing it the children are becoming a part of them. And it is marvelous. Something that is going very well. They have opened nurseries in the *barrio* where the little ones are cared for while the mothers look for life [earn a living]. It used to be that the children were abandoned [left alone to fend for themselves], but now many are cared for in what is like a school. And there they give them food . . . and all those things.
>
> For that reason, the parents are changing too. Because little by little they see that improvement . . . the education being given their children. And when the

"While the mothers look for life . . ."

children return home, for example, and let's say hear the parents speak some great blasphemy, the children say, "Papa! Papa! That is not said! You don't speak that way!" . . . And that way the children correct the parents. And the parents see that—and it fills them with joy to see the children teaching them. They know that the children are better off, even though they work less for their support. The parents recognize it as a true and good work of people who invest their time without self-gain. And without doubt this leads to progress, and this is very good, very good.

Interviews with La Chana's Gypsies failed, however, to substantiate the marked optimism reflected in Pepe's view of progress in the *barrio*. While some of the Gypsies feel less isolated in La Chana, others (older residents) continue to look to the Sacro Monte as their home. In spite of La Chana's low rents, approximately 90 *pesetas* ($1.50) per month for three rooms, they are bitter about the extension into permanency of what they had believed to be a temporary move. Blame for not repairing damaged caves was variously attributed to corrupt officials and to the greed of local residents eager to use the Sacro Monte for touristic purposes only. While charges were phrased in vague terms, there was, nevertheless, a sense of exploitation and anger in their expression. Among the Gypsies who found life easier in La Chana was a *gitana* who noted that, "As poor as our homes are, they are not flooded." Parenthetically, she added, "We have more water here, and do not have to carry it so far."

The education of children in the *barrio* nursery was seen as valuable more in terms of food and medical aid provided by the school than in the context of educational advantage. A visit to the nursery school revealed that it consisted of a small building with a fenced-in, gravel-covered yard. Some little shade was provided by thatching at one end of the open enclosure. There appeared to be approximately one hundred children in the nursery. No toys or furniture were visible. The children played in groups, alternately resting on the ground. Freed of worry for very young children during working hours, poorer Gypsy parents accepted the fact that the school lightened parental burdens, but appeared to be disinterested in the program's long-range goals.

Gypsy families in La Chana continue to suffer from hunger, and our small gifts of money to children more frequently than not were used for bread, rice, and milk for the family table rather than for the ice cream for which they were intended. The desire for a "better life" continued to be Gypsy centered in actual fact, and we did not find among adults much evidence of either rapid or significant change in their life style. Questioned about changes since moving to La Chana, Gypsy informants vehemently denied that they were *"importante."* The picaroon is still apparent among them, and we were entertained endlessly by tales of recent tricks played upon the credulous *payo*. "To be a Gypsy is in the blood wherever we live," said one *gitano* with indulgent good humor. He obviously regarded our question as naïve in the extreme. Some of the changes that have taken place are indeed "plenty good," but they primarily affect the very young and the more prosperous Gypsies. They have yet to manifest themselves in distinguishable ways among the majority of La Chana's *gitanos*, in spite of their recognition of church and volunteer efforts as "a true and good work."

The few instances reported of Gypsies who continue their education beyond

Barrio family

middle-childhood years (some who have become teachers, a Gypsy physician, and the like) were cited by Señor Pino as illustrative of the fact that education, religion, and tourism are raising the aspirations of some Gypsy families. In these very rare instances, Gypsy students were reported to have unusually high intellectual ability when compared to their non-Gypsy peers. The fact is, however, that very few children attend school at all.

Similarly, the traditional Gypsy elopement is disappearing among the better-educated and/or more successful Gypsy families, being replaced by the church wedding "in white" for which our child informants expressed such strong desire. In addition, the marriage age among this minority group is tending to more closely approximate the Spanish norm of twenty to twenty-seven rather than the Gypsy norm of fifteen to seventeen. But these changes, like the ability of some Gypsies to speak a little French, English, and/or German, are apparent most among Gypsies whose contacts with non-Gypsies are characterized by frequency and intimacy—in Granada, those who engage in the flamenco arts either as *zambra* proprietors or as recognized artists. They are far less pronounced even among the Gypsies of La Chana who are employed as *jaleadores* or as lesser performers in the *cuadros*. "A more modern life" is translated among this larger group as better housing, the wish for clothing, the desire for food on the table. "Some of our customs change," said one Gypsy, "but we lag many years behind."

"We Make League Even with Dogs"

Gypsy/non-Gypsy relationships in Andalusia have been characterized by a greater degree of tolerance and understanding than is found either in Spain's northern provinces or in other countries of the world.

It is in Spain that the Gypsies, or rather the *gitanos* have found one of their most favorable homes. In fact, and only after centuries of repression, they have gained almost complete freedom which only the Gypsies of Britain (and the United States) need envy. At a time when, in the rest of Europe the nomad remains a pariah, subject to coercive and vexatious measures, the Spanish *gitanos* are perfectly integrated in the Spanish population, especially in Andalusia (Clébert 1963:203).

While the Gypsy status in southern Spain has been transformed until today he has come to occupy an enviable position there, the case for "perfect integration" is difficult to support in fact. Convergencies in Andalusian and Gypsy culture have facilitated contacts between the two groups, but both continue, with rare exceptions, to view themselves as apart, distinct. The traditional mandate of Gypsies to maintain separateness from non-Gypsy populations and their pride in "race" both function to delay rather than advance the integrative process. Intermarriage is strongly discouraged, albeit such unions tend to meet with less drastic measures today than in the past. The acceptance of the *payo*, however, is governed by the degree to which he subordinates his own traditions to those of the Gypsies. The daughter of one such union, it will be recalled, said of her *payo* father, "He has lived among *us*," clearly indicating the Gypsy/non-Gypsy dichotomy still recognized by them. In housing, too, Granada's Gypsies remain, for the most part, in self-segregated *barrios*. The desire for a "flat down in town," like education, a church wedding, and so forth, is expressed only by more successful Gypsy families. In the two instances with which we have been intimately associated of Gypsy artists who made such a move, both continue to spend more time in familial *cuevas* than in their apartments. Said one, "I see my friends in the Sacro Monte and it fills me with envy." While it is doubtless true that the Gypsy, more than the Andalusian, rejects "perfect integration," the receptivity of Andalusains to Gypsies is by no means characterized by nonprejudicial attitudes. A *gitana*, in discussing these relationships, described both personal and professional problems arising from contacts with "*castellanos*."

I don't know what we have inside of us—*we make league—even with dogs.* We relate to everyone because we let everyone live. If someone does something bad, we don't attach importance to it. And that way we don't have envy nor hatred. Even if someone is bad, we keep quiet. After all, what can we do? Some have heavier burdens, some lighter. And ours is a good life. We get along well.
But sometimes there are people who think that a Gypsy is inferior to them. They think that Gypsies are less than they are. They think that Gypsies have superstitions, for example, that they are afraid of snakes, and they taunt them. On purpose, they bother the Gypsies. [*Note*: While strongly denying fear of snakes, the informant avoided use of the word *serpiente* throughout her narration. Upon direct questioning, she displayed great uneasiness, substituting instead the word for bug. For purposes of clarity we have used the correct term in her recitation of a recent incident she had experienced in town.]
When I got into the bus, a man upon seeing me started to say, "Oh, that serpent,"—and this and that and I don't know what else. And my husband knew that these comments were directed at me. And because that had happened once before, in another bus, he thought that it was the same man. He said, "Doesn't it shame you—you, without education, without dignity. If I had you outside, I'd leave you there" [He would kill him]. He said, "Don't you see that my woman

is with *me*?" Then the man said, "I didn't mean to say anything bad," and my husband said, "You said it because my wife is a Gypsy, and you are trying to bother her by mentioning those snakes—but you cannot scare her with that. Instead of the serpent frightening her, it will strangle you!"

And for reasons like that, there are some Gypsies who do not get *in* with *castellanos*. There are people, *payos*, for whom the Gypsy has no appeal. And there are many Gypsies to whom the *payos* do not appeal. And there are *payos* who lose their lives to Gypsies. And there are Gypsies who marry *payos*. Same thing. There are people in Spain who don't like Negroes and some who don't like Jews, and some hate Gypsies. They don't like them because they say, "At best, the Gypsy is this and that." They say, "Gypsies are not the same as we are." And then there are others who say, "I don't see any difference between us." And we get along very well. We don't always fight. On the contrary, we are the same.

In spite of the informant's assertion, "We are the same," the ethnocentrism of Gypsy culture is unconsciously underlined in her boast, "We make league— even with *dogs*," that is, non-Gypsies. The sense of helplessness shared by most minority groups, manifests itself in Gypsy dependency upon maintaining the good will of the very people who take advantage of their minority status. Another informant observed,

In the past, before the good dancers left the Sacro Monte, private groups would come to see the *zambras*. Each person paid at least 100 *pesetas* to us. Now, with the agencies, we earn 25 *pesetas*, or less. And our good dancers leave. Some of the tour guides spread propaganda that it is safer to travel with the tour because "Gypsies may rob you or attack you with knives, and fight with you." Right in front of us they tell the people that we are very dangerous, and we must keep our mouths closed—or lose the business.

The sense of outrage of this informant at unfounded accusations directed at Gypsies, and their economic consequences, were reflected in our three-generational study of the current concerns of Gypsies engaged in the flamenco arts.

"*Mal Tiempo*"

Tangible manifestations of greater Gypsy security are somewhat misleading in terms of the Gypsy's self-view of his current prospects and hopes for the future. A television count, for example, is hardly revealing of what people of different cultures and circumstances are feeling, albeit it may be a temporary measure of material achievement or satisfaction. As rising wants and aspirations tend to outstrip actual acquisition and realization, the lag between the two appears to be widened rather than narrowed. Wishing to preserve the Gypsy way, his expectations, aspirations, and fears are caught up between the press and pull of the minority world of which he is a part and the majority world upon which he is dependent.

Use of Hadley Cantril's Self-Anchoring Striving Scale, including its nonverbal ladder device, permitted us to study the effects of circumstances on the outlooks which a family of *gitanos* held for themselves and for their group, as

well·as to acquire insight into the nature of the conflicts they face. While de-
limited to a particular family and occupational group, the key position and influence of these Gypsies—that is, employment of other Gypsies, the high regard
in which they are held in the Sacro Monte and La Chana, and their close contacts
with segments of Granada's non-Gypsy population—lend to their statements a
greater degree of significance than might be suggested by this delimitation. They
are subjective statements of how certain of our Gypsy informants actually feel
about their lives, but they address themselves to the larger cultural context, revealing
some of its shared hopes and fears, its continuities and discontinuities. Responses
to questions concerning what "really matters" in life, and how an imaginary
"perfect" future might look, were both modest and traditional in nature:

> What I aspire for in life is that things work out for each person, so that all
> can pursue life.
> That my family have no bad illnesses.
> That my health would get better so that I am able to lead, to sing, and to
> have my Gypsy art.
> To have the joy of youth in old age.
> I don't ask for grand things, only the means of life, and the *alegría*.
> I want things to progress—that each day improves, and that many tourists
> come.
> To be able to see my grandchildren grow up.

The immediacy of Gypsy aspirations was expressed by a young *gitana* who
saw her life now as she would wish it to be in the future. "My life *is* happy. I have
my parents, they live and are not sick. My child too, has good health. I have my
husband, my grandparents, and what's more, I am expecting another child. I
don't see how I could desire more. Do you understand? I consider my life, at this
very moment, happy." When pressed further, she added, "I would like my child
to be educated, to have a future—things we have not been able to have." This
same informant's fears were also child centered, and tended, like those of other
informants, to focus on death. "I am worried that the same thing that came with
my daughter [the death of her twin] will happen again. That they [her expected
child] will be two, and that God will take away one."

The worst possible form the future could assume was viewed in terms
of loneliness, loss of independence, and that "bad things"—war—might come again
to Spain.

> I do not want to be alone. I do not want my husband to die, but rather want
> us to grow old together. To have a little *peseta* here and there, so that no one
> has to give us food.

> I would like to die without seeing anything else bad. I speak the truth. I
> would like for there to be goodwill among all people. That cannot be when
> there are ugly things.

As indicated in the last response, fears were not infrequently phrased as
wishes, and two informants demonstrated impatience with our attempt to cate-
gorize answers in terms of "best" versus "worst," and wishes versus fears. Said
one, "Naturally they are but the reverse of one another. Not to have my wishes

in reality is what I fear the most. It is not necessary, therefore, to answer more than once."

In locating themselves on Cantril's ladder device, that is, at present, five years ago, and five years from now, informants displayed certain inconsistencies

$$
\begin{array}{c}
\underline{10} \\
\underline{9} \\
\underline{8} \\
\underline{7} \\
\underline{6} \\
\underline{5} \\
\underline{4} \\
\underline{3} \\
\underline{2} \\
\underline{1} \\
\underline{0}
\end{array}
$$

in explaining their choices. For example, the *gitana* who saw herself as "happy now" placed herself at a lower rung in the symbolic "ladder of life" because "now I have my husband, my child, my home, and all those responsibilities." Five years previously she placed herself four rungs higher, at the top. "I was freer. My life was very good. I danced in the *zambra* and was happy." In another five years she indicated that she thought she would be one step from the top, as her children would be older and she would be adjusted to her home responsibilities. However, the fact that her husband did not want her to dance in the *zambra* appeared to preclude her achieving her earlier high.

The informant's grandmother placed herself at the present time on rung 3, close to the bottom of the ladder device, saying, "*Mal tiempo, mal tiempo.* We have had a bad winter, and my husband was very sick." Five years ago, she, like her granddaughter, was four rungs higher, although not at the top of the ladder. "I felt better. I could work more." Her optimism for the future was based on family loyalties, but did not embrace Gypsy welfare in general. A *zambra dueña*, she saw welfare threatened by current changes in the culture and in the decline of *zambra* earning power.

Both her husband and her daughter saw their lives as more quiet now. However, whereas the husband placed himself at step 8, the daughter saw herself currently at step 4 only. Her movement from rung 3 to 4 in five years was attributed to improvements in her personal life (health) and to new conveniences added to her cave home. Her five-year projection for herself included a four-step movement in which she envisioned herself enjoying a better personal life with her grandchildren. Her father, like her mother, held to the hope of a better personal future, but differed in anticipating a similar degree of progress in Gypsy culture.

Gypsies most closely associated with *zambra* activities and responsibilities tended to be most pessimistic about group welfare. In using Cantril's questions, we substituted Gypsy culture for "country" in an attempt to identify group hopes, fears, prospects. The high degree of integration of work, play, and tradition in Gypsy culture, and its pragmatic orientations, yielded such answers as:

> Life was better five years ago before the floods. More Gypsies lived in the Sacro Monte, and more good artists worked in the *zambras*. We had more tourism [earned more from private groups].
> More artists now work in nightclubs and hotels. It is harder to live our Gypsy life. Some sons now do not return to their mothers.
> It is harder today for Gypsies engaged in the arts to find enough *duros* to live well.
> The *alegría* of life, the arts, those things were better then than now.

Seeing occupational threat, as well as disruption in familial and economic loyalties, the daughter projected a downward trend in Gypsy welfare and saw the culture as moving in five years from its present rung 6 position on the ladder to a low rung 3. These concerns, anchored, as Cantril has noted, in the individual's reality world, were echoed by her mother, who said, "The Gypsy way was good for us. It was as it should be, not like now." Conversely, younger members of the family saw the culture as advancing, and projected, through more education, better health care, and the possibility of Gypsies engaging in other occupations, an increase rather than decrease in overall group welfare. The sharing of this optimism by the grandfather was dismissed by both his wife and daughter as "an old man's dream."

It is difficult to compare Gypsy concerns with those of people of the so-called developing nations or of the urbanized world, though they have moved and lived among them for centuries. This is not to say that their concerns do not converge with those Cantril identified as universal to human beings everywhere (1965:315–322), such as the satisfaction of survival needs, the sense of physical and psychological security, hope, the need for personal dignity, and "to present myself as a person."

The Gypsy has exaggerated certain basic uniformities in the human design, making ends out of means, and investing them with a sacredness that defies radical change. Habitual behavior for the Gypsy is not a springboard for "takeoffs in new directions" but rather is a value in itself. Fear of alienation, the desire "to be as we are *now*," the focus on short-term goals, usually defined in traditional terms—all of these recurrent themes in life history and other materials present a picture of a society deviating in basic ways from norms derived from the study of either urban or "emerging" peoples.

Plugged into the changing world, the Gypsy with few exceptions remains traditionally *not* future oriented, looking instead to the present or the past for directionality. He rarely asks, "Where am I going?" in the sense of transforming his life style. In many ways he wants to "stay put," borrowing from those around him only those things which he perceives as relevant to the Gypsy way. His materialistic bent tends to be misleading; the television set does not replace face-to-face communication in his society, his world of things remains subordinated to his world of persons.

Whereas few people in Cantril's study were "self-consciously concerned with freedom as a category in the code," our Gypsy informants continuously verbalized the value of this theme in their culture. Maintained antithetically by tradition, the Gypsy concept of freedom influences their occupational choices, relationships with non-Gypsies, spending and recreational patterns. The *alegría* of Gypsy life, its emphasis on pleasure, whim, extreme expression of emotion, all are sanctioned by the conscious sharing of this cultural theme. At the individual level, however, the traditionalism of Gypsy culture operates as a brake on free choice, its freedoms being tightly constrained within the framework of group custom.

American Culture: A Gypsy View

In an unique and anthropologically rare instance, several of the Gypsy informants with whom we have worked in southern Spain—dancers, singers, guitarists—were brought to the 1964–1965 New York World's Fair for performances at the Spanish Pavilion. In a reversal of roles, they became the students of culture, ours, and we—their subjects. Now we were *it*, and they, acting as "natural" ethnopsychologists, probed, questioned, observed, and participated for six months in a culture they unscientifically but obviously regarded as barbaric, inferior, "primitive," and lacking, for all of its luxuries, in the know-how to live the good life.

Nonchanging aspects and values of Gypsy culture are both implied in their observations about American culture and made explicit through data subsequently recorded in Granada and Madrid.

"*All Americans do is make money. They know little about how to live. They honor only those things others have made. Most create nothing.*" The integration of the arts in Gypsy life, that is the fact that they service materialistic, enculturative, and personal needs—"the singer sings first of all for his own consolation"—coupled with the Gypsy honoring of highly personalized, face-to-face relationships, were reflected in their reaction to the utilitarian, "dehumanized" aspects of American life. Creativity in science, engineering, and technology was dismissed as "practical" but as distinctive from "true art." As has been noted, in addressing their own hopes and fears, Gypsies display a high degree of selectivity in the choices they make, reworking borrowed elements so that they fit into the framework of tradition. The lack of family-centered loyalties—"your children go away"—the spectator role of Americans in their relationships to the arts, and the rapid pace of urban life, all were regarded as inferior to the Gypsy way.

"*You rush, rush, rush. You applaud what others say is good, but you do not take time to know whether it is good or not.*" This observation was made in terms of American audiences who wildly applauded *zambra* performances the Gypsies felt to be mediocre and lacking in *duende*. To "rush" and, therefore, not to "know" was viewed as a waste, and is a negation of the *alegría* they see as characteristic of their own life style. Their own materialism and opportunism were viewed as servicing only their basic survival needs in order that they might continue to pursue their Gypsy life with its wit, conversation, and "*una copita* of sherry to help the song along." Television sets and other modern conveniences were shrugged off as not necessary but nice to have—"the things that matter are food on the table, and the *joy*, the *joy*. You Americans are too serious, and forget this." This refrain was echoed by a *gitana* in Granada in 1968 who said, "You know that Gypsies don't always have enough food to eat, which is the most important thing. But, even so, they never lack *alegría*. What is best about Gypsy life is its joy. This they will never lose."

"You are children without mothers." The anomic life style of urban Americans was seen by our Gypsy observers to preclude meaningful human relationships, and to minimize rather than maximize the individual in his psychocultural context. The absence, in their view, of what Redfield called a "design for living" was attributed by them to account for the chaos and disorders in American culture, with which their hotel television sets had familiarized them. To be without mothers, as this recurrent theme in their culture emphasizes, translates among them to mean "rootless," devoid of shared understandings, meaningless. The strong sense of belonging together in Gypsy society was seen by them to be transformed in our urban world into impersonal, bureaucratic, ever-shifting patterns of human relationships which, least comprehensible of all to them, even included members of one's own kin group.

The observation that *"even your children do not know how to play"* was directed at both the seeming absence of artistic creativity in mass culture and its tendency to homogenize its young according to formalized school norms. The dependency of American children on manufactured toys, the rigid scheduling of childhood hours, and age grouping and its concomitant discontinuities appeared to them to rob our children of free play and spontaneity. Segregated in the world of childhood, they asked, "When do your children learn to be adults, to know life?" *"In America, children and adults are too far apart. It seems they do not like each other."* The direct experience of Gypsy children with their cultural heritage, a heritage communicated verbally, through the folk arts, and largely in an intimate face-to-face milieu, was not, in their opinion, mirrored in American culture. Seeing our children as "victims" of an impersonal school system, isolated from the adult world, they saw them as failing to acquire that sense of being linked to the past which, without benefit of written history, strongly unites each generation of Gypsies one to the other. "We want just a little schooling. . . ."

Watching news telecasts of the Watts racial riots led one young *gitano* dancer to state, *"You have many laws, but no law. Gypsy laws are few, but we live by them. This does not seem to be your way."* Working on the assumption that rich and poor people are subject to different legal norms, Gypsy visitors identified closely with racial problems in the United States, an identification based primarily on what they viewed as inconsistencies in the application of law. "You say this, but you do that. How can this be?" We have been similarly questioned in subsequent field trips to Spain concerning violence in American culture. "You kill all of your best people. Los Kennedys, Martín Lutero King. *Es una locura* [it is a madness]. *What you do not understand, you mistreat."*

The all-pervasive American cultural norm, *work*, defined, as it appeared to our Gypsy informant/observers, in terms only of visible activity, one-dimensionally, as it were, brought forth the observation that *"Unlike you, we do not sell ourselves, but we are cleverer than most in these matters. What you think, and what is true sometimes are not the same."*

The continued subordination of work to other Gypsy values—family loyalty, pleasure, freedom, and so forth—and their selective adaptation to Andalusian culture, in which similar values are found, was sharply contrasted by them to our state of perpetual motion and anomie. Liking the generosity of Americans, they pitied their inability to "take time to enjoy life—people." The exaggerated ethnocentrism of Gypsy culture was expressed most strongly in their sense of "cleverness" at being able to work and to indulge their strong materialistic wants without being dominated by either. While Gypsy and American materialism appear to converge, they are divergent in the priorities assigned them in their respective cultural systems. Similarly, individualism in both cultures—the honoring of style, achievement, and the like—is linked to quite different motivations in each. For the Gypsy, the idealized son is one whose individual achievement contributes to *group* welfare and pride. The American image of the self-made man has little appeal to the Gypsy, nor does independence from kin group seem "natural" to them. The fear of aloneness, alienation from the group, is shared by even its most deviant members, and is a cause for cultural stress in contemporary Gypsy life.

The fatalism of Gypsy culture, its passions, its loyalties, operate still to maintain a relatively balanced state within the culture. While the cumulative effects of change on some of its traditional affiliation patterns, themes, and associations have produced stress areas in the culture, one of its striking features continues to be its sense of positive self-identity. Internalized and shared, the affective regard of Gypsies for their "way" causes them to reject aspects of urban life which, to them, appear destructive and self-limiting. *"We know how to make happiness out of grief. You, who have so much, work so hard at being happy that you are not. We have little, but this knowledge we have."*

Going about in our midst and "reading our secrets," Gypsy observations about American life are both harsh and lean. Their primary significance in this chapter, which has devoted itself principally to aspects of change, is that voiced as they were by the most acculturated members of *zambra* families, they underscore unchanging rather than changing values in their culture. Seeing Americans in their own backyards, they returned, as one informant noted, "to Granada, to our Spanish land, to our *cuevas*. That is our joy."

Distorted, seen from a limited perspective, the Gypsy view of American life may have little validity for us. We are reminded, however, of a photograph sent to some Gypsy friends in Granada. At the time requested, the only one available was ten years old. Back came an acknowledgment. "Thank you for the photograph. My, you have aged!" No gloss, no flattery. That blunt statement of truth caused a hasty retreat to the mirror.

8

Pulling It Off

THIS BOOK STARTED with the question, "What is a Gypsy?" In attempting to answer it, we have depended upon a combination of methodological approaches. The observant/participant techniques of the ethnologist were utilized for a period spanning a decade of work in Granada's Sacro Monte. More recently, the use of Cantril's Self-Anchoring Striving Scale, and the study of children's wishes provided data relevant to changing aspirations and wants. Revealing cultural and "subjective standards which guide behavior and define satisfaction or frustration" (Cantril 1965:21), these data were supplemented by frequent recourse to life history materials. Especially in interdisciplinary work does the life history (which offers a valuable methodological common denominator for behavorial scientists) yield data essential to understanding the individual in his culture and culture change. As noted by Langness,

> The problems of current anthropological investigation demand a reorientation of methodology to keep pace with the shifts in interest, and this reorientation must be in the direction of more sensitive insights into the individual actors. There would seem to be at present no adequate substitute for the life history (1965:51).

In this summary chapter, we present the individual actor as creature, carrier, and creator/manipulator of his culture. Using Simmons' definitions of these terms (1967: 388–389), Gypsy informants are viewed as they reflect their culture, as they exemplify and transmit it, and, finally, as they innovate or manipulate within its constraining framework. The last viewpoint includes data concerning individuation and stress and some possible cultural consequences of activities which appear to be transcendent rather than adaptive to the culture.

The Gypsy as a Creature of Culture

The deep internalization of Gypsy culture by its participants, and the conscious and subconscious mirroring of its norms, approved forms of behavior, and traditional belief systems continued to be apparent in even our most recent field experiences. As a creature of his culture, the Gypsy continues to live in the "here and now," little knowing or caring about his historical past or his historical future. Physically strong, dynamic, and vigorous, his acting out of the

Gypsy way is characterized by the same extremes of passion that mark his human relationships. Fiercely loyal, aggressive, and proud, the Gypsy deals primarily in *feelings*. The statement "I sing for you not because you are intelligent but because I saw that you could *feel* the song" illustrates the priority assigned to the ability to engage in intense emotional, rather than intellectual involvement. The stamp of Gypsy culture bites deeply, with the result that its practitioners share many common elements of personality, which enables them to see themselves reflected in the actions, attitudes, and beliefs of the group of which they are a part. This sense of mirrored familiarity, of belonging, manifests itself not only in exaggerated group ethnocentrism but also in strong positive self-images. The high esteem in which Gypsies hold themselves as compared to outsiders is one of the core characteristics of the Gypsy personality. It has functioned in the past to enable him to survive, curiously without bitterness, inhuman persecution and deprivation; indeed, to thrive in spite of them. Through his belief in Gypsy superiority—without recourse to heroes or figures of great legendary import, the individual comes to view *himself* as hero. Although he lives on the fringes of history, he lives there as a hero in his own eyes, proud and aloof.

The elements of Gypsy culture best known to outsiders—his unconventional dress, myths concerning his occult powers, begging, and other defiances of Western convention—have acted to delay outside penetration into his society. Feared and distrusted, the Gypsy has been content to utilize and, at times, to foster these attitudes in others in order to preserve his own uniqueness. Rejecting values of the urban, technological world (thrift, serious attitudes toward work and responsibility, cooperation, science), he clings tenaciously to his concepts of freedom, "alegría," fatalism. Vacillating from extremes of joy to deep, tragic sorrow, from passionate affection to violent aggression, he maximizes with immediacy and spontaneity his loves and his hates. Guilt feelings are minimized by the fact that his behavior is both shared and approved within his society, provided that he does not violate its traditional laws. Confined as he is to his own closely knit group, he holds the values of the *payo* in contempt and, therefore, is not significantly affected by them. The cohesiveness of Gypsy society facilitates self-acceptance and a strong sense of identity. Until recently, anomie was virtually unknown except among Gypsies ostracized from the group by their dreaded Gypsy tribunals. As a creature of his culture, shrewdness and wit, and intuition rather than a priori reasoning, dominate in the Gypsy's dealings with outsiders. Highly perceptive, his survival dependent upon accuracy in judgment, the Gypsy has come to excel at sizing up the *payo* in the service of his own interests. Fearful of solitude, he has clung to the society of which he is a product, honoring its traditions and transmitting them to his children.

The Gypsy as a Carrier of Culture

The high degree of visibility of Gypsy vanity (his carriage, hauteur, disdainful gaze) may be viewed as representative of his effectiveness as a culture carrier. Not only does he convince himself of his own superiority but, not infrequently, he convinces us of it too! In intimate communication with his children, permitting them almost total participation in the adult world, and lavishing praise upon them for acts and attitudes reflective of Gypsy traditions, the Gypsy, by precept and example, transmits and perpetuates the Gypsy way from one generation to the next. "My son," proudly stated a young *gitano* to us recently, "is like the skin of the Devil." This phrase translates to mean that the child is mischievous—"with the salt of God"—in other words, that he manifests in his behavior the kind of male aggressiveness Gypsies encourage.

Word of mouth was observed to dominate as the principal means of communication, in spite of the ability of some Gypsies to read and write and the presence of radios and, more recently, television sets in some of the homes of Granada's sedentary Gypsies. Concomitantly, the use and function of folk songs and other art forms were found to focus in part upon enculturative interests which stressed the preservation and transmission of traditional culture themes.

As manifest in Deep Song *coplas*, the themes of familial and ethnic loyalty were reinforced not only by songs of praise but by those illustrative of the penalties

"Pharaoh's daughters":
carriers of
"the Gypsy way"

and sufferings occasioned by their denial as well. *Coplas* telling of the persecution and durability of Gypsies were found to be rooted in an historical past in which violence and cruelty were not uncommonly sanctioned by Spanish law. Less frequently sung in public, these *coplas* enjoined the Gypsies to remain apart from the dominant Spanish community and to direct all loyalty and energy inward in support of group interests. Other culture themes expressed in the *coplas* include freedom, ethnic superiority (often expressed in terms of "royal blood"), preeminence of Gypsy law, and fatalism. In spite of noting some weakening trends, all informants pointed out that the songs continued to teach "obedience to the Gypsy way."

In summary, Redfield, more than twenty years ago, attributed the retention of the characteristics of a folk society by Gypsies (1947), in spite of their movement among urbanites, to precisely the type of oral communication pattern found operative in Andalusia during the five-year period spanning 1959 to 1964. In essence, Andalusian Gypsy society continued to be a familial society in which conservation of tradition was of paramount importance, in spite of selective adaptation to new demands of contemporary life. Believing in an innate Gypsy "style," the Gypsy, as a culture carrier, views as inevitable the perpetuation of his traditions, occupations—"the babies come out dancing"—and ethnic identity. "*It is in the blood. . . .*"

The Gypsy as Creator/Manipulator of Culture

It is more difficult to see the Gypsy in the role of creator of culture than as its creature or carrier. The conservative ethos which operates as a brake on change, the honoring of tradition, and the frequent recourse to his own uniqueness—"We do not throw away the light of life. That's how we are different from you."—all tend to mask the ways by which he has innovated within his cultural confines. Yet, as revealed in the preceding chapter, Gypsy adaptation to Andulsian norms evinces a steady, albeit highly selective, progression from almost total rejection to a rather comfortable acceptance of new ideas and artifacts which service his interests. Innovative, for example, in terms of utilizing his traditional metalworking arts in the production of new items reflecting contemporary Andalusian tastes, and shrewdly capitalizing on his tourist-attracting value, the Gypsy has increased his economic potential. He rejects most Western values:

> We do not sell ourselves—but we are cleverer than most in these matters.
> You earn money, and say I'll save this for that and that for this. *We* earn a thousand *pesetas* and spend it. We do not worry about tomorrow.

Yet he has successfully manipulated some of them to his own advantage. Permitting his children to acquire basic literacy skills and exposing them to Catholic teachings, his focus shifts from the Western view of long-range achievement to the Gypsy view of short-range advantage, such as free lunches for children, childcare services, outwitting non-Gypsy business associates.

Like most traditional peoples caught up in change, the Gypsy, at once comfortable with new material satisfactions, lives uneasily with their consequences. Studies conducted during the past six years have revealed growing conflicts between traditional affiliation patterns described as characteristic of Andalusian Gypsy culture and the aspirations of its individual members. Trends were isolated indicating the weakening of Gypsy social controls as fuller participation in the affairs of the dominant community is tolerated.

The thematic content of the culture appears to be undergoing modification in terms of individual rather than group goals or, more accurately, modifications which *include* individual as well as group interests. Concomitants of this trend are an increase in intragroup tensions, a growing sense of individual alienation, and the threatening of the economic cohesion of the family unit as its more gifted and/or younger members tend to disassociate themselves from direct participation in its maintenance and welfare. As has been noted, among Granada's performing Gypsies the increased movement of the best of the dancers, singers, and guitarists out of the Sacro Monte, attracted by the higher wages to be found in the cities or "on tour," is reported to have had severe effects upon the earning power of the Gypsy families engaged in producing *zambras* for visiting tourists. Engagements which are either prolonged in nature or which involve travel, coupled with rising aspirations in terms both of individual recognition and material wants, are seen to weaken the tradition of exploiting superior individual talent for the benefit of the family as a whole. In other words, the previously reported distinguishing feature of Gypsy culture—its highly developed ability to select from the outside world those features which could easily be integrated into the existing cultural framework or utilized without disturbing its basic affiliational patterns—appears to be changing as new aspirations of its individual members conflict with its traditional laws and loyalties.

Seen by older informants as negations of Gypsy law with its deceptively simple yet all inclusive precepts, slowly evolving trends toward integrated housing, economic independence, and more rarely, intermarriage are cause for cultural concern which transcends by far the relatively few instances of actual transgression reported. Variously attributed, in order of importance indicated, to the influence of tourism, technological progress, and education, key informants of sedentary Sacro Monte families nonetheless tended to support the view of an elderly chief that "in the end, the Gypsy way always endures." Even among younger informants, some of whom deviated in their own life styles from group norms (by, for example, "living below in the town") there was a strong tendency toward continued idealization of cultural tradition. In general, they viewed their own deviations merely as expedient and/or temporary in nature, and attempted to reduce anxieties related to the fear of alienation by justifying them in terms of group rather than individual welfare.

Features of Gypsy society not supportive of individual autonomy (the reverse of Goodman's urban findings, 1967:226) include: the small size of its population; the lack of cultural bulk as measured in terms of a multiplicity of skills and ideas; the strong press of its traditions; its lack of literacy; its homogeneity; its dependence on informal enculturative processes; and its fatalistic orientation. Experiencing "high frequency and varied interpersonal contacts" with urbanites, the Gypsy nevertheless remains apart from them, retaining and nurturing the "folkness" of his culture and personality. Accordingly, the pull toward autonomous action is minimized, albeit existent. The price paid by the individual for acting in autonomous or transcendent ways is apt to be high, occasioning conflict and stress in the group.

Whether contemporary signs of stress and individuation in Gypsy culture will bear out Borrow's prediction of their utimate assimilation by the larger non-Gypsy population (1908) or will serve, as in the past, to reinforce their cultural tenacity remains to be seen. The unquestioning loyalty of most Gypsies to their laws and traditions has been credited with having enabled them to maintain their ethnic distinctness during former periods of persecution, chaos, and change. However, this is not to say that Gypsy society is a static one. Even in the matter of law, in spite of the unchanging nature of the precepts themselves, its interpretations tend toward greater flexibility under the influence of cultural advances made in the dominant non-Gypsy community. As Spanish law has been humanized, Gypsy dependence on civil justice has increased. Similarly, the fuller acceptance of Catholicism coincides with the more sympathetic attitude adopted by the church toward the Gypsy. In rare instances, even intermarriage is accepted, provided that the non-Gypsy partner remains subordinate to members of his Gypsy family and contributes significantly to their welfare. In these ways, Andalusian Gypsy culture, more specifically that of Granada's sedentary Gypsies, may be compared in its dependence upon the city for new ideas and artifacts to Spanish rural culture as described in the works of Pitt-Rivers (1954) and Kenny (1966).

Subordinate to urban influence, and often misinterpreting its trends, the coexistence of contradictions in Gypsy culture is readily apparent to its students. Distrusting formal education, but seeing advantage in basic literacy skills; deploring individuation, yet desiring the material rewards which may accompany it; demanding obedience to the Gypsy way, but honoring actions characterized by innovative style; idealizing *alegría*, yet, in reality, working very hard; Gypsy culture enjoins its members to make use of what the urban world has to offer. At the same time, its traditional dynamic operates to constrain individual autonomy which threatens established social controls and affiliation patterns. As with Deep Song styles, improvisation within the framework established by tradition has been both tolerated and encouraged historically. In the meantime, however, new ways are as "discomforting" to the Gypsies of Granada today as they have been reported to be to the villagers of Ramosierra (Kenny 1966:234).

Further comparisons may be drawn from the assumption that in neither Gypsy nor peasant culture is the reworking of newly diffused elements likely to keep pace with trends in urban Spain. Lacking political and economic influence, as well as education, the resultant phenomenon of cultural lag operates both as a brake on progress and to maintain itself in folk and peasant culture. As recently restated by Foster, "Time to simmer is an essential part of the concept of peasant [folk] culture, time to integrate diffused traits and complexes into the peasant [folk] fabric, to rework them and to make them harmonious with the functional whole" (1967:11).

What may prove to distinguish Gypsy from peasant adaptation to change, however, is the opportunistic orientation and thrust of Gypsy culture and the tenacity of its historical insistence upon cultural uniqueness. *The Gypsy wants to remain a Gypsy.* Well-practiced in the art of dealing with diverse cultures and peoples, the Andalusian Gypsy may just pull it off!

Glossary

Aficionado: A flamenco connoisseur; possessing knowledge and deep intuition.
Alegría: Gypsy joy; merriment.
Alegrías: A gay type of Andalusian song and dance.
Baile: Dance.
Barrio: District; quarter; neighborhood.
Bulería: Improvised fast Gypsy songs and dances; full of gusto; ideal for Gypsy *juergas*.
Calés: Spanish Gypsies.
Caló: Language of Spanish Gypsies.
Cantaores: Folk singers.
Cante flamenco: Andalusian folk song; light textured; Gypsified. Also known as *cante chico*.
Cante jondo: Deep Song; the most profound and ancient song form of Andalusia; also known as *cante grande*.
Castellano: Castilian; as used by Gypsies, "Spaniards."
Copla: Folk poem or song.
Cuadro: Team of flamenco performers.
Cuevas: Caves.
Debla: A super *martinete*; ancient song sung without guitar.
Dicha (La):   Luck.
Dueña: Proprietress.
Duende: Demon; soul or spirit in folk music.
Fandango gitano: Song and dance of Arabic origin; danced "freely" by Gypsies in Granada.
Feria: Fair; holiday.
Flamenco: Flaming; Gypsified; lively; Andalusian dance or song.
Gitanería: Gypsy quarter; district.
Gitano (A):   Spanish Gypsy.
Gracia: Grace; cleverness; charm.
Hado: Fate; destiny.
Hombría: Manliness.
Jaleador: Beat setter; one who encourages dancers.
Juerga: A spree; Gypsy revelry.
Kris: Gypsy justice; tribunal.
Malagueña: Flamenco song of Malaga.
Mantón: Fringed shawl.
Martinete: Song of the forge; *cante grande* of Gypsy metalworkers.
Novio (A):   Bridegroom; bride; suitor.
Olla: Gypsy stew; pot of boiled meats and vegetables.
Patrin (pateran):   Gypsy trail sign; secret symbols used to guide nomadic Gypsies.
Payo: Non-Gypsy; frequently denigrating; also *Busno, Gadjo; Gorgio*.
Picaroon: A roguish "hero"; one skilled in flattery and persuasion.
Pitos: Snapping of fingers in Gypsy dance.
Rom: Man; husband; Gypsy.
Siguiriya gitana: Weeping song; among the oldest and purest of *cante jondo* forms.
Soleares: Songs of solitude; primitive archetype of *cante jondo*.
Saeta: An "arrow" of song; heard during Holy Week.
Zambra: Revelry; a night with songs and dances in the moonlight.

References

BERCOVICI, KONRAD, 1928, *The Story of the Gypsies.* New York: Cosmopolitan Book Corporation.

BLOCK, MARTIN, 1939, *Gypsies—Their Life and Their Customs.* New York: Appleton-Century-Crofts.

BORROW, GEORGE, 1842, *The Bible in Spain.* Great Britain: T. Nelson & Sons, Ltd.

————, 1908, *The Zincali, An Account of the Gypsies in Spain.* New York: G. P. Putnam's Sons.

BROWN, IRVING, 1922, *Nights and Days on the Gypsy Trail.* New York: Harper & Row, Publishers.

————, 1929, *Deep Song.* New York: Harper & Row, Publishers.

CANTRIL, HADLEY, 1965, *The Patterns of Human Concerns.* New Brunswick, N.J.: Rutgers University Press.

CHASE, GILBERT, 1941, *The Music of Spain.* New York: W. W. Norton & Company, Inc.

CIMORRA, CLEMENTE, 1943, *El Cante Jondo.* Buenos Aires: Editorial Schapire.

CLÉBERT, JEAN-PAUL, 1963, *The Gypsies.* New York: E. P. Dutton & Co., Inc.

ELLIS, HAVELOCK, 1926, *The Soul of Spain.* London: Constable & Co., Ltd.

FALLA, MANUEL DE, 1950, *Escritos Sobre Música y Músico.* Buenos Aires: Espasa-Calpe Argentina, S. A.

GARN, STANLEY M., 1961, *Human Races.* Springfield, Ill.: Charles C Thomas, Publisher.

GOODMAN, MARY ELLEN, 1967, *The Individual and Culture.* Homewood, Ill.: The Dorsey Press.

GRELLMANN, HEINRICH, 1807, *Dissertation on the Gypsies: With an Historical Enquiry Concerning Their Origin and First Appearance in Europe.* London: William Ballintine.

GROPPER, RENA C., 1967, "Urban Nomads—The Gypsies of New York City," *Transactions,* New York Academy of Sciences, series II, vol. 29:1050–56.

HARRISON, JAMES A., 1903, *Spain.* Akron, Ohio: The Sealfield Publishing Company.

HOEBEL, E. ADAMSON, 1954, *The Law of Primitive Man.* Cambridge, Mass.: Harvard University Press.

————, 1966, *Anthropology.* New York: McGraw-Hill, Inc.

HONIGMANN, JOHN J., 1961, "North America," in *Psychological Anthropology: Approaches to Culture and Personality,* Frances L. K. Hsu (ed.), Homewood, Ill.: The Dorsey Press.

HSU, FRANCIS L. K., 1969, *The Study of Literate Societies.* New York: Holt, Rinehart and Winston, Inc.

HULSE, FREDERICK S., 1963, *The Human Species.* New York: Random House, Inc.

HUMPHRIES, ROLFE (trans.), 1954, *The Gypsy Ballads of García Lorca.* Bloomington: Indiana University Press.

KEESING, FELIX M., 1959, *Cultural Anthropology.* New York: Holt, Rinehart and Winston, Inc.

KENNY, MICHAEL, 1966, *A Spanish Tapestry.* New York: Harper Calophon Books, Harper and Row, Publishers.

KROEBER, A. L., 1948, *Anthropology.* New York: Harcourt, Brace & World, Inc.

LAFUENTE, RAFAEL, 1955, *Los Gitanos, El Flamenco, y Los Flamencos.* Barcelona: Editorial Barna, S. A.

LANGNESS, L. L., 1965, *The Life History in Anthropological Science.* New York: Holt, Rinehart and Winston, Inc.

LOMAX, ALAN, 1959, "Folk Song Style," *American Anthropologist* 61:927–54.

LORCA, FEDERICO GARCÍA, 1957, *Poema del Cante Jondo.* Buenos Aires: Editorial Losada, S. A.

LUNA, JOSÉ CARLOS DE, 1952, *Gitanos de la Bética.* Madrid; Ediciones y Publicaciones Españolas, S. A.

MADARIAGA, SALVADOR DE, 1958, *Spain, a Modern History.* New York: Frederick A. Praeger, Inc.

MILLER, TOWNSEND, 1964, *The Castles and the Crown.* New York: Capricorn Books.

OCAÑA, JUAN SANCHEZ, 1963, *Granada y Sus Gitanos.* Granada; Escuelas del Ave-María.

OPLER, MORRIS E., 1945, "Themes as Dynamic Forces in Culture," *American Journal of Sociology* 51:198–200.

ORTEGA y GASSET, JOSÉ, 1937. *Invertebrate Spain.* New York: W. W. Norton & Company, Inc.

PITT-RIVERS, J. A., 1963, *The People of the Sierra.* Chicago: University of Chicago Press.

POTTER, JACK M., MAY N. DIAZ, AND GEORGE M. FOSTER, 1967, *Peasant Society, A Reader.* Boston: Little, Brown & Company.

PRITCHETT, V. S., 1954, *The Spanish Temper.* New York: Alfred A. Knopf.

QUINTANA, BERTHA, 1960, *The Deep Song of the Andalusian Gypsies; A Study of the Transmission and Perpetuation of Traditional Culture Themes.* Doctoral thesis, (L.C. Card No. Mic. 60-3775). New York: New York University.

REDFIELD, ROBERT, 1947, "The Folk Society." *The American Journal of Sociology* 52:293–308.

————, 1957, *The Primitive World and its Transformations.* Ithaca, N. Y.: Cornell University Press Great Seal Book.

SAMPSON, JOHN (ed.), 1930, *The Wind on the Heath, A Gypsy Anthology.* London: Chatto and Windus, Ltd.

SIMMONS, LEO W. (ed.), 1967, *Sun Chief, The Autobiography of a Hopi Indian.* New Haven: Yale University Press.

SPINDLER, GEORGE D. (ed.), 1955, *Education and Anthropology.* Stanford, California: Stanford University Press.

STARKIE, WALTER, 1935, *The Gypsy in Andalusian Folk-Lore and Folk-Music.* London: The British Musical Association.

————, 1937, *Don Gypsy.* New York: E. P. Dutton & Co., Inc.

————, 1953, *In Sara's Tents.* New York: E. P. Dutton & Co., Inc.

————, 1957, *The Road to Santiago.* New York: E. P. Dutton & Co., Inc.

————, 1958, *Spain: A Musician's Journey Through Time and Space.* Vols. I, II. Geneva, Switzerland: EDISLI--At Editions Rene Kister.

TORNER, EDUARDO M., 1944, "La Canción Tradicional Española," *Folklore y Costumbres De España.* F. Carreras, Editor. Barcelona: Casa Editorial Alberto Martin.

UN MAESTRO DE DICHAS ESCUELAS, 1946, *Vida de Don Andrés Manjón y Manjón, Fundador De Las Escuelas Del Ave María.* Imprenta Tallereo Penitenciarios De Alcalá de Henares.

VILLAJOS, C. G. ORTIZ DE, 1949, *Gitanos De Granada.* Granada: Editoral Andalucia.

YOORS, JAN, 1967, *The Gypsies.* New York: Simon and Schuster, Inc.

Recommended Readings

BLOCK, MARTIN, 1939, *Gypsies—Their Life and Their Customs*. New York: Apple-
ton-Century-Crofts.
> An important contribution to the study of Gypsy history and culture; a pene-
> trating and scholarly work; well illustrated.
BORROW, GEORGE, 1908, *The Zincali, An Account of the Gypsies in Spain*. New
York: G. P. Putnam's Sons.
> England's "Romany Rye" was one of the early chroniclers of Gypsy culture.
> Living in close contact with them, his classic account of Spanish *gitanos* (first
> published in 1841) remains one of the best sources of their history, folklore,
> and songs. Borrow's insights into the psychology of Gypsy life styles served
> to stimulate the development of gypsiology in the nineteenth century.
BROWN, IRVING, 1929, *Deep Song*. New York: Harper & Row, Publishers.
> A personalized account of the author's intimate contacts with Spanish Gypsies
> and their music; contains one of the most complete collections of Deep Song
> *coplas* in print.
CLÉBERT, JEAN-PAUL, 1967, *The Gypsies*. Baltimore: Penguin Books, Inc. (paper-
back edition).
> A comprehensive study of Gypsies of the world. Tracing probable lines of Gypsy
> migrations, the author moves from early dispersals to the position of Gypsies
> in contemporary societies.
ESTY, KATHERINE, 1969, *The Gypsies: Wanderers in Time*. Des Moines, Iowa: Mere-
dith Press.
> A well-written book containing summarized historical data about Gypsies;
> chapters on twentieth-century problems, and Gypsies in America are especially
> noteworthy.
GROPPER, RENA C., 1967, "Urban Nomads—The Gypsies of New York City," *Trans-
actions*, New York Academy of Sciences, series II, vol. 29:1050–56.
> This paper reflects its anthropological author's twenty years of actual observation
> of New York City's Gypsy populations; contains an excellent analysis of the
> structuring of Gypsy society, its value system and ideals.
KENNY, MICHAEL, 1966, *A Spanish Tapestry*. New York: Harper Calophon Books,
Harper & Row, Publishers (paperback edition).
> An outstanding study by a cultural anthropologist of Spanish village life, its
> continuities and discontinuities as contrasted to a Madrid parish.
PITT-RIVERS, J. A., 1963, *The People of the Sierra*. Chicago: University of Chicago
Press (paperback edition).
> An exemplary ethnographic description and analysis of Andalusian rural life;
> contains interesting data about village attitudes toward Gypsies and their customs.
STARKIE, WALTER, 1937, *Don Gypsy*. New York: E. P. Dutton & Co., Inc.
> One of Starkie's best accounts of his life on the Gypsy trail; as with all of the
> author's works, this book is highly readable, describing with vivid detail his
> experiences as scholar and minstrel among Spain's *gitanos*.
———, 1953, *In Sara's Tents*. New York: E. P. Dutton & Co., Inc.
> Focuses on Starkie's pilgrimage with Gypsies to the shrine of Sara, patron saint
> of the Romanichals. Great figures of literature, art, and music are encountered
> along the way, together with colorful Gypsy personalities—bullfighters, *flamenco*
> artists, nomads. The chapter on "The Flamenco Caste" is one of the finest written
> about the Gypsy contribution to Spanish music.

————, 1957, *The Road to Santiago*. New York: E. P. Dutton & Co., Inc.

More encounters with Spanish Gypsies as Starkie crosses the Iberian peninsula enroute to Santiago de Compostela, the burial place of St. James, patron of Spain. This work reflects its author's remarkable knowledge of Spain's people and places, all of which are treated with sensitivity and insight.

YOORS, JAN, 1968, *The Gypsies*. New York: Simon and Schuster, Inc. (paperback edition).

In this fascinating account of a Belgian boyhood spent as a member of a nomadic Gypsy horde, its author succeeds in his stated purpose. "I want to evoke a mood . . . of the simple dignity of the Rom."

JOURNAL OF THE GYPSY LORE SOCIETY. (Liverpool: The University Library.)

The quarterly publication of the Gypsy Lore Society. Founded in 1888 for the purpose of improving the quality of Gypsy studies, the *Journal* publishes accounts written by its scholarly members; without qualification, the best source for materials about Gypsy customs, language, folktales, contemporary status, and so forth. Walter F. Starkie, C.M.G., has been president of the Society since 1961.